James Edwin Thorold Rogers

Historical Gleanings; a Series of Sketches

Montagu, Walpole, Adam Smith, Cobbett

James Edwin Thorold Rogers

Historical Gleanings; a Series of Sketches
Montagu, Walpole, Adam Smith, Cobbett

ISBN/EAN: 9783337098940

Printed in Europe, USA, Canada, Australia, Japan

Cover: Foto ©Thomas Meinert / pixelio.de

More available books at **www.hansebooks.com**

HISTORICAL GLEANINGS

A SERIES OF SKETCHES

MONTAGU. WALPOLE. ADAM SMITH.
COBBETT.

BY

JAMES E. THOROLD ROGERS

London
MACMILLAN AND CO.
1869

[*All rights reserved*]

OXFORD:
BY T. COMBE, M.A., E. B. GARDNER, E. P. HALL, AND H. LATHAM, M.A.,
PRINTERS TO THE UNIVERSITY.

PREFACE.

THE object which I have before me in the following sketches, is to present a set of historical facts, grouped round a principal figure. The essays are in the form of lectures. Three out of the four were read at Newcastle-on-Tyne, before the Philosophical Society; and at Rochdale, before the Pioneers. The fourth, the subject of which is Walpole, was read to an audience in University College, London.

The history of the eighteenth century ought to have greater practical interest in the eyes of Englishmen than that of any other epoch in their annals. During this time, the political system of the country grew up, despite the imperfections which characterised the machinery of Parliament and the scandals which accompanied nearly every administration. The same century witnessed the growth of national wealth, in the expansion of this country's commerce and manufactures, despite the erroneous economical theories which found acceptance with most thinkers and almost every statesman. That negative side of politics and economy which gathers its inferences from the refutation of persistent fallacies, and which therefore assists towards dissipating other delusions, which are not yet abandoned, was developed in the first instance from the practice and the theory of the same age.

If any writer could draw a series of sketches, which might enable the general reader to arrive at a clear conception of the social and economical condition of our immediate ancestors, he might make truth as entertaining as fiction, and be instructive as well as agreeable. To effect such a result, he will need certain powers. He must have skill in grouping his facts, as well as the art of lively composition. But the chief part of his labour will consist in the collection of materials.

I can lay claim to no higher merit than that of diligent collection. I cannot assume that I have made the subjects which I am treating in the following pages as clear to my reader as they are to myself. But I am persuaded that the writer who possesses the gift of historical exposition, might follow the method pursued in these sketches with advantage, and thus make the past live again to his reader.

I have not undergirded my pages with a single note; have not cited the host of authorities to whom I am indebted for my facts. There is, I think, a tiresome affectation in such a cumber of references, when the originals are open to the study of all. If I had to serve up a heap of strawberries on one dish, I see no reason why I should gravely present my guest with a heap of stalks on another dish.

I make no apology for the economical reasonings which are interspersed in these lectures. In treating any historical topic it is necessary to acknowledge wars and dynastic combinations, but the best part of historical teaching does not, I think, consist in the more prominent events which have occupied the attention of those who lived among such facts or who were their agents, but in expounding the moral and material progress of society, and thereupon such parts of history as are too customary to attract superficial attention. It is very rarely the case that persons are able to form a just estimate of the time in which they are living. It is certain that the only means of arriving at even an imperfect estimate is to be obtained by a survey of society from its economical aspect.

JAMES E. THOROLD ROGERS.

OXFORD, *June* 5, 1869.

CHARLES MONTAGU,

EARL OF HALIFAX.

CHARLES MONTAGU,

EARL OF HALIFAX.

In 1658, these islands were a great republic. Cromwell's administration made Great Britain more powerful in Europe than it had been since the days of the warrior Plantagenets. But the task which he had completed was in the highest degree arduous. The stars in their courses fought against him. His government was revolutionary, and therefore costly. He had enemies among his own partisans, for many of his companions in arms envied his elevation, not a few, more honestly, believed that Oliver's protectorate was a mischievous and indefensible usurpation. He was in daily peril of his life from his acknowledged foes. The stories told about the gloomy anxiety of the great Protector's later years, malignant as they probably, exaggerated as they certainly are, are indirect testimony of the ceaseless plots which threatened him. Cromwell's reign was marked by a succession of bad seasons, under which the nation was afflicted with severe dearth. But the throne of no monarch was, if one may judge from the respect in which he was held, more glorious than his Highness' chair of state. He constrained all

European monarchs to acknowledge him. He even arrested the arm of the Inquisition in the valleys of the Southern Alps. Charles, whom he had driven into exile, would have entered into negotiations with the illustrious usurper—would have even allied himself with the principal author of his father's death. It is known that Cromwell suspended, or broke off these negotiations, because he believed that the royal wanderer would never forgive the great enemy of his house. But the exiles of a dynasty very rarely preserve their self-respect, and Charles Stuart was the least respectable among all the exiles of history. He wanted nothing but ease and pleasure, and we all know what his ease and pleasure were.

Thirty years after, the Revolution occurred, and a limited monarchy was established. There was an interregnum of two months between the day on which James fled from the kingdom, and William was proclaimed. We are told by more than one authority, that the republican party, which forty years before had overthrown the monarchy and the Church, was wholly extinct. Such a phenomenon has never been witnessed before. The war of American independence settled at once and for ever the form of political institutions in all new communities of Anglo-Saxon origin. The principle of social equality has survived all the other dogmas of that revolutionary propaganda in France which began its mission a century after the English settlement. But the great Puritan movement of the seventeenth century exhausted itself in the effort which gives it its place in English history. Like the volcanos of Auvergne, it burnt itself out. The government of the Protector is as purely historical as the constitution of Athens or Rome. It is even more historical, for the traditions of ancient civilization still enter into modern habits of political thought. The stock arguments against republican institutions have been handed down from the days of Plato. The code of ancient Rome is the core of European law. But the policy of the Protectorate is, in so far as its influence on political thought goes, infinitely more archaic than that of the republics of the ancient world. At the close of the seventeenth century, people thought that the republication of Milton's Iconoclastes was an impertinence, and languidly asked whether it was likely to serve the present establishment in Church and State.

For the fact is, no reaction was ever so absolute as the change from the era of the Rebellion to that of the Restoration. The heroes of the former epoch were earnest, stern, precise. Their sincerity was attested by the persecution which they had endured. Their discipline was perfected by the struggle in which they ultimately conquered. The purpose of their opposition to the King and his cavaliers must have been plainly before them, if not from the day of Eliot's imprisonment and slow murder, at least from the time that Charles raised his standard at Nottingham. The character of the King made the struggle desperate, even unto death. Charles, like his son James, never forgave. But he was infinitely superior to his son in finesse, or as a less courtly critic might say, in duplicity.

It is not easy to discover the extent to which the nation took part in the great civil war. But it is certain that the real combatants were few. Before the armies joined battle at Naseby, it is said that a party of country gentlemen crossed the field with their hounds in full cry. Charles wondered that any of his subjects could be neutral on that day. It was the neutrality of these men which restored the monarchy. Had the same impulses, the same passions which moved Roundhead and Cavalier moved every Englishman, the victory of the former would never have been followed by reaction.

If it be necessary to illustrate this statement, that the great Puritan party was numerically small, no better proof, I think, can be found than the fact that the capitular and episcopal estates, sold in the early days of the first revolution at fair market prices, were resumed for their ancient owners after the Restoration, without compensation. I know no parallel instance of this resumption. Henry the Eighth's courtiers secured their grasp on the abbey lands, despite Mary's desire that they should be restored. Similarly, after the restoration of the Bourbons, it was impossible to recover the Church, or even the lay estates in France, which the Revolution had confiscated and sold. A revolution must be superficial indeed which cannot secure a permanent title to its grantees.

It was because the leaders of the republican party were few, and were trained under such exceptional circumstances, that they had no successors. The party was inevitably weakened by the efflux of time. Had the ague, which carried Cromwell off at a comparatively early age, been cured; had his life been prolonged to the general duration; his own comrades would have passed away, and his son would have succeeded to a quiet hereditary throne. This event was indeed in course of fulfilment. Never were Charles' prospects worse than at the beginning of the year in which Oliver died.

Meanwhile the clergy, whom Cromwell was obliged to conciliate, were alienating the laity by their dark fanaticism, their harsh discipline, their intolerant zeal. A statesman who affects to be a defender of the faith, is invariably unfriendly to public liberty. Never since the Reformation was the State so much the handmaid of the Church as during the early days of the Protectorate. Men found that they had exchanged the tyranny of the High Commission Court, of which they had heard, but of which they had rarely had experience, for a prying parochial inquisition, which controlled their daily life. These unrecorded grievances were far worse than the occasional persecutions of the monarchical courts. The English people has never submitted to clerical government as patiently as the Scotch has. What that government was, may be seen in the diaries of Cotton Mather and Shepherd, the ministers of the Massachusetts settlement under Governor Winthorp, the men who burnt witches and hanged Quakers by the score. The harshness of the Presbyterian discipline was peculiarly galling to persons who might have otherwise acquiesced in the Protectorate. There were few who mourned for the ejected ministers of Bartholomew's Day 1662. The doctrine of these godly men might have been pure, but the managers of the Hampton Court Conference, the Morleys and Sheldons, were wiser in their generation, when they restored episcopal government, and with it the jolly, genial parson; and in place of the Kirk Session the Act of Uniformity.

As the State and the Church of the Protectorate were exceptional, so was the Court of the Restoration. At least let us, for the sake of human nature, hope so. The Cavaliers who formed the retinue of Charles, as he lived anxiously at Breda, were as starved as they were licentious. Charles himself was familiar with penury. It is said that he had even experienced famine, and that he retained after his restoration a strange fondness for putrid oysters, because this happened to be the dish with which he had once satiated the cravings of his hunger. These ravening and unclean creatures, when their master returned to England, flew upon the spoil like vultures. Charles' court was one vast revel, a perpetual round of debauchery. It contained no modest woman, no honest man. Everybody remembers the description which Evelyn gives of the last Sunday of Charles' life. It was a feast of Cotytto, a worship of

Ashtaroth. Everybody knows Pepys' diary and the prudish gossiping way in which he tells the story of social life in England. But the annalist of these revels, the most polished among the satyrs and blacklegs and bullies of the restored throne, was Grammont. No writer gives a clearer picture of the scene at Hampton and Tonbridge than this creature does. Those who can touch pitch with gloved hands may read his book, and may learn how gross was the pollution in which the nobles of the day wallowed, and from which they were very slowly reclaimed. Where is the contrast to this picture? As Milton lived in Cripplegate, blind and poor, he must have realized in the court, Comus and his retinue, the first creation of his prophetic genius, as he drew, half unconsciously, in the most sublime and characteristic of his works, his own portrait, under the name of Samson, blind and with shorn locks, a captive grinding in the prison-house of the Philistines, while his persecutors were 'drunk with idolatry, drunk with wine.'

Charles the First and his son after him, had robbed the London merchants, the former of the money which they had deposited in the Mint under the guarantee of Government, the latter of what was an enormous sum in those days, no less than £1,328,526, and which lay in the Exchequer. Charles shut up the Exchequer, but promised to pay six per cent. on the principal which he had appropriated, as long as it was unpaid. It is hardly necessary to say that this promise was broken. No interest was paid for thirty years. But at the beginning of the eighteenth century the government of William effected a compromise. The creditors of Charles agreed to take three per cent. on the principal, the Government stipulating that they might redeem the debt on paying half the sum which had been seized. This, the oldest part of the National debt, for it is the only portion which was contracted before the Revolution, is still one of the public liabilities. But more than ten thousand families were ruined by this robbery. The motive for the act was as rapacious as the act was ruinous.

Charles was in constant want of money. His pleasures, and the accidents of these pleasures, needed sustentation, the former immediately, the latter by permanent provision. But Parliament, whose loyalty was rather ardent than self-denying, was slow to gratify him, and inquisitive in its grants of supplies. Even in the first burst of affection which gushed forth at the time of the Restoration, the Cavaliers relieved their estates from feudal charges, as Cavaliers have done before and since, by levying taxes on the general public. They commuted the aids and reliefs, which constituted the conditions of the estates which they enjoyed, for the hereditary excise. The malt tax of the present day represents the expedient by which the landowners of the Restoration freed themselves from their ancient contributions to the public revenue.

As Parliament was unwilling to assist him, Charles, who shrank from no baseness, became the willing pensioner of Louis XIV. The price paid for this pension was the declaration of war against Holland. Charles was willing, in order to gain the means for gratifying his infamous pleasures, and for maintaining the wild orgies of his Court, not only to make war on his own nephew, but to assist in the attempted subjugation of the Dutch provinces, then, as a century before, the bulwark of the Reformed Religion. Fortunately, the attempt was frustrated. The defeat and dishonour which attended the English arms, when our fleet was burnt in the Medway, and our efforts against the heroic defenders of Amsterdam were foiled, saved the English people in the end. It is a small matter to add, that Holland had given Charles an asylum during the days of the terrible Protector, where he could intrigue, and where, when he had funds, he could hire his assassins in safety. It was only after years had passed that William of Orange learnt the terms of the bargain which Charles had made with Louis, and the plot which was intended to compass his destruction. It is not marvellous that he felt little compunction in dispossessing a kinsman who had taken part in these intrigues, especially as he knew so well that the safety of Europe depended on the chastisement of Louis.

The reaction of immorality during the age of Charles the Second was so complete that even men of otherwise stainless character were open to purchase. There is one name indeed, that of Lord Russell, on which no charge of corruption can be fastened. But Sidney seems to have been in the pay of Louis. Mr. Hallam gives an odd justification of this relation between the French autocrat and the English republican. He claims a moral distinction between a bribe taken to betray our principles, and a present taken in order to maintain them. One would think that under these abnormal circumstances, there must at least have been a sympathy between the giver and the receiver, and we know that there could have been no honest sympathy between Louis and Sidney. But the truth is this. When men walk with their lives in their hands, as all public men did in England during the days of Oates and Dangerfield on the one hand, Scroggs and Jeffries on the other, they become strangely heroic, or as strangely base. Of the former class were Russell and Essex, of the latter Shaftesbury and Marlborough, and a host of other men. Most of the difficulties which William and his better supporters had to contend with arose from the men who had been trained in that perfidious school.

There is no need that I should dwell in these prefatory remarks on the short and stormy reign of James the Second. Very few parts of English history are better known to Englishmen than the three years of that reign. The base Parliament of 1685, is remembered as the most infamous in our annals. James did everything to shock what loyalty was left towards the House of Stuart. He might indeed—

for monarchs live in strangely constructed houses, in which more is seen of them than is the fact, and less is always known by them—have thought that the loyalty of that University of Oxford which accepted the dedication of Sir George Mackenzie's Jus Regium, and endorsed it with their famous anathema on the twenty dogmas, which they pronounced to be false, seditious, and impious, was beyond suspicion of change. In 1709, the House of Lords reversed this Academical judgment, by ordering the decree to be publicly burnt by the common hangman.

James may have counted on this loyalty. But loyalty, amid the strife of factions, is a phrase which denotes satisfaction at that course of policy which rewards adherents. Loyalty, indeed, was entertained towards the House of Stuart, but it was to be found among the gallant savages of the Highlands, among the desperate and persecuted outlaws of Irish bogs and mountains. When James attacked the freehold of the fellows of Magdalene, and threatened the High Church partisans with the Indulgence, these sturdy advocates of his divine right fell from him, like autumn leaves in a tempest. Nor was this all. The disaffection of those who have been loyal, is incomparably more dangerous than the plots and sedition of those who have always been dissatisfied. The London Gazette of February 1688 is full of congratulatory addresses on the birth of the Prince of Wales. The London Gazette of February 1689 is as full of congratulatory addresses to William and Mary. Whigs and Tories who acquiesced in the new settlement, agreed in branding that child, whom a few months before they had welcomed as a choice gift from Heaven, as supposititious, and in charging James with a fraud, of which, with all his faults, he was incapable. In his subsequent career, the old Pretender proved his legitimacy, by exhibiting all the characteristic incompetency, bigotry, and obstinacy of the House of Stuart.

James, after his exile began, had a singular body of adherents. He had imprisoned the bishops for disobedience, and they had been acquitted. After his enforced abdication several of the prelates, with a considerable body of followers, declined to take the oath of allegiance to the new Settlement. It became necessary to dispossess them, a step which William was very reluctant to take. But they were treated with great, and I may add, with well deserved leniency. Though they were not loyal subjects, they were peaceable. If their principle of passive obedience dissuaded them from vowing allegiance to William, it equally precluded them from active co-operation in Jacobite plots. This harmless secession, which seemed at first so dangerous, survived for more than a century. Surprise has been expressed at its tenacious vitality. But travellers in the United States tell us, that there are small communities of American citizens whose settlement is two centuries old, but who have never cast a vote—passionate as is the habit of voting throughout the Union — because the President has never adopted the Solemn League and Covenant.

The real danger which the Revolution of 1688 ran, was the astonishing treachery of the principal men in the State. Much of this was due to the school in which public men had learned, not a little to the conduct of William himself, his harsh manners, his attachment to his Dutch troops, his intense and inconsiderate partiality for his Dutch courtiers and favourites. William ennobled and enriched the house of Bentinck, a house which has been traditionally characterised by a stubborn and unforgiving will, but he intended to have heaped grants on his favourite with a prodigality which would have made him the richest subject, if not the richest personage in Europe. But the inveterate depravity of the nobles at the Revolution was William's chief difficulty. Various as the characteristics of these men were, they were at one in their greed, their dissimulation, and their perfidy. Such men as Marlborough, Admiral Russell, Godolphin, Carmarthen, were able and willing to paralyse any policy. It was due to such men as these that better terms were not got at the peace of Ryswick. It was because William was surrounded by such a crew that he was constrained to become his own minister, and to insist on a larger prerogative than any constitutional king has subsequently exercised. It was to counteract these persons that William discovered and used the services of those men who were faithful to him and his policy, and among them of Charles Montagu, afterwards Baron and Earl of Halifax.

When Shakespeare is describing the ragged regiment with which Falstaff declined to walk through Coventry, because even he was disgraced by so beggarly a militia, he reckons among his hundred and fifty tattered prodigals 'discarded serving-men, revolted tapsters, ostlers trade-fallen, younger sons to younger brothers,' and speaks of them as 'the cankers of a calm world and a long peace.' What was true of the younger sons of younger brothers, when military employment was not to be had, in the days of Shakespeare, was true in the days of William the Third, was true in Normandy eighty years later still. The only refuges for these victims of primogeniture were the army and the church. They did not expect command in the army, for many a gentleman of ancient descent, but impoverished substance, trailed a pike as a common soldier at Steenkirk and Landen, or at the siege of Namur. The Anglican Church, nearly two centuries ago, offered very little better prospects. It was impoverished at the Reformation, and has become wealthy, if indeed endowments make it wealthy, from subsequent accidents. At that time however, the parson, and especially the chaplain, got the income of the butler, and was thought lucky if he married the lady's maid of his patroness, or some lower dependant of his patron. He is the perpetual jest of the dramatists of the age, the Wycherleys, and Congreves, and Vanbrughs, for his servility and his shifts, for his poverty and his clumsy attempts to ingratiate himself with his patrons. It has been noticed that the only man of good descent and substance who had taken orders between the Reformation and the Revolution, was Henry Compton, Bishop of London, who had been a cavalry officer, and who for a while reassumed that position at the Revolution, riding at the head of the guard of honour which escorted the Princess Anne to a place of safety, when she deserted her father in the autumn of 1688.

The younger sons of the French nobility were better off up to the time of the French Revolution. The custom of primogeniture was not so strictly followed in France. The riches of the Church too were still unimpaired, and persons of good descent regularly took orders, and were nominated to abbacies. There is a story told of Turgot, the teacher and predecessor of Adam Smith, that when he had resolved again to become a layman, and abandon his prospects in the Gallican Church, his friends remonstrated with him. 'You are,' they said, 'the younger son of a Norman nobleman, and therefore are poor. Your father is a man of great reputation, your relations are men of influence, and you will speedily be nominated to excellent abbacies. You will soon become a bishop. As easily you may be translated to a better see, as for example in Provence or Brittany. You will thus be able to realise your dreams of administrative usefulness, and, without ceasing to be a churchman, may be a statesman at your leisure.' It is needless to say that these ecclesiastics did little credit to their profession. One of them, expelled from France for his extraordinary profligacy, singular even in the bad age which I have described, became the tool, the spy, and at last the would-be murderer of Harley. But the Abbé Guiscard was by no means a unique scoundrel.

In 1688, the Church was the only prospect before Charles Montagu. His father was George Montagu, his grandfather was the first Earl of Manchester. He was the fourth son of nine children. Born in 1661, he was sent to Westminster at fourteen, then and for many years before and afterwards ruled by the famous Dr. Busby, who diligently instructed the minds, and ruthlessly cudgelled the bodies, of the ingenuous youth of the period. At sixteen, he was elected a King's scholar, at twenty-one he was sent to Trinity College, Cambridge. It appears that his choice of University was determined by his attachment to a schoolfellow. At all events, he was fortunate. Had he gone to Oxford, he could have been sent to Christ Church, under the discipline of Dr. Fell, Dean and Bishop of the see of Oxford, a strenuous partisan of the Divine right of Kings and of passive obedience, and the advocate of the famous decree to which I have already alluded. As it was, he went to Cambridge, and became the pupil, as he was afterwards the patron, of Sir Isaac Newton.

It may be mentioned that he constantly lived on terms of friendship with the great philosopher, and that he left him a legacy in his will, 'as a mark,' in his own language, 'of the honour and esteem he had for so great a man.'

At Cambridge, Montagu cultivated what was called poetry, as young men even now write rhymes at the Universities on set subjects. It appears that the trick of verse-making never left him, and that he tagged couplets together, and built up Pindaric odes to the day of his death. At least so Walpole says, who is our best authority for the gossip of that time. Never perhaps was English poetry at a lower ebb. Milton had no followers, no admirers even. He could have had no imitators. The poet of the age had been Cowley, it was Dryden. Justice is still done to the vigorous style and active genius of that eminent writer, whose slovenliness in versification only was imitated by his disciples. After Dryden's death, Swift could quote almost every living versifier in order to illustrate his essay on the art of sinking in poetry. Few however of these poetasters were worse than Montagu. He was a generous man, and he patronized the rhymesters, as Lord Palmerston did Poet Close. Intending to honour him with their gratitude, Grub Street inserted his compositions in its manifold collections of the British classics. It was a cruel kindness. My audience will be able to judge of Montagu's merits as a versifier from a few specimens.

His earliest poem, written, it appears, at the request or command of the Cambridge authorities,—Trinity College is a royal foundation, and therefore officially puts on Court mourning,—is on the death of Charles the Second. There is little variety in the language which is used to extol the merits of deceased princes; but our young poet was guilty of an inexcusable flattery when he writes of Charles as

> 'The best good man that ever filled a throne;'

and speaks of his 'awful person,' when we know that the excessive ugliness of his face was relieved only by his habitual expression of good temper. Subsequently he compares him to the Almighty and King David, and describes the political enemies of his youth as Sauls, who were 'made great by wandering asses.' In a similar strain he tells us that 'the flying towers, with canvas wings,' by which he means the mercantile marine of the day, whose development he most unfairly ascribes to Charles, are the means by which the English

> 'In Persian silks, eat Persian spice, secure
> From burning fluxes and their calenture;'

a couplet in which one is at a loss which to admire the most—the conceit, the geography, or the physiology. He concludes his poem by saying—

> 'James is our Charles in all things but in name;
> Thus Thames is daily lost, but still the same.'

Five years later, Montagu's maturer powers were employed in congratulating William, in even worse verses, on the victory of the Boyne. Thus he writes about the passage of the river—

> 'Precipitate they plunge into the flood;
> In vain the waves, the banks, the men withstood:'

and of William—

> 'The King leads on; the King does all inflame;
> The King—and carries millions in his name.'

I will make but one more quotation, his description of Mary—

> 'As danger did approach, her spirits rose,
> And, putting on the King, dismayed his foes.
> Now, all in joy, she quits the cheerful Court;
> In every glance descending angels sport.'

This, you will agree with me, is sad stuff, and only worthy of a prosaic economist. I know but one apology for it, that in those days Locke professed a profound admiration for the genius of Sir Richard Blackmore.

There is one composition, the joint work of Montagu and a far wittier person, Matthew Prior, which will live side by side with the poem which it parodies. When Dryden joined the Roman communion, he testified his gratitude to James, and his attachment to his new creed, by composing a poem, the conception of which is transcendently absurd, though the execution is as meritorious as that which characterises any other of Dryden's works. Under the figure of a Hind and a Panther, the converted wit and man of letters typified the Roman and the English Churches.

The Hind invites the Panther to her cave, and there discourses on Church history, discipline, and dogmas, on the authority of general councils, of kings, and of the Pope. The Panther, who ought to be convinced, goes away unconverted; and, instead of being so gnawed by the pangs of hunger during this long and tedious lecture as to devour her fellow-controversialist, leaves the milk-white Hind civilly and harmlessly. Never was fable composed which was open to more measureless ridicule. It was travestied by Montagu and Prior under the title of The Town and Country Mouse. This performance gained Montagu the friendship of Lord Dorset, and opened him a career, when he was still hovering between the rival misery of the Church and the Bar.

About ninety of the Upper House of Parliament, some being bishops, all who had sat in any Parliament of Charles the Second, the Lord Mayor and about fifty of the Common Council, met on December 26, 1688, after the King's flight, and requested the Prince to issue writs for the summons of a Convention Parliament. To this Convention, which met on January 22, Montagu was returned, and in this Convention the abdication or forfeiture of King James was formally affirmed; William and Mary were invested with the Crown. We may be certain that the young statesman acquitted himself well, for the King forthwith presented him with a pension of £500. For a time, this was the way in which the Court rewarded its adherents in Parliament. The severity which debars the recipient of a pension—some few cases excepted—from sitting in the House of Commons, was adopted in order to check this practice. The expedient—one of the days of Queen Anne—was only outwardly successful, for Walpole contrived to obtain and secure partisans by the distribution of secret bribes.

When Montagu was thirty years old he managed a conference of the Commons with the House of Lords. Both political parties in the Legislature, not the least, probably, because of the insecurity of the new settlement, were anxious to define anew the law of treason, and to enact an amended course of procedure. Up to this time, that terrible law had been administered after the statute of Edward the Third, corrected by another of Edward the Sixth, and expounded by the practice of some of the very worst judges in the very worst times. The trials of Lord Strafford and Archbishop Plunket, on the one hand; of Russell, Sidney, and College on the other, in the time of Charles the Second, were murders carried out under forms of law, and in defiance of plain justice. It was everybody's interest to amend the written law, and to define anew what should be the practice of the Court. The Lords insisted on securing some special privileges to their order; the Commons demurred, and Montagu, as I have said, managed the conference. For a time, the dissentients could not agree, and the bill was lost. Ultimately, however, the Lower House conceded the demands of the Upper.

The skill which Montagu exhibited in this and similar kinds of public business, his readiness in debate, and his painstaking, methodical manner, soon marked him for that kind of official life, skill in which was absolutely necessary for the support of the Revolution, skill of which at that time he was the sole master. Montagu was the father of English finance. He pledged, and pledged successfully, the public credit. He furthered the project which established the Bank of England. He thwarted Harley and the Tories in their attempt to degrade the currency in 1695. But his greatest effort of financial genius was the happy audacity which invented and circulated Exchequer bills.

It is a saying of Macaulay, that public debts were not contracted for the first time at the Revolution; but that the responsible Government which commenced at that epoch commenced also the practice of paying them. Henry the Third borrowed of the Pope, then and for generations afterwards, the greatest capitalist in Europe. Edward the Third borrowed of the Genoese and Florentine merchants, and failing to pay, ruined these traffickers. The later Plantagenet and the Tudor kings borrowed of their subjects and repudiated their debts. Twice in his reign Henry the Eighth, the most lavish and reckless of English kings, was relieved of his debts by Parliament, taking with grim pleasantry the benefit of the Act. When these resources failed, Henry debased the currency, and dragged this country down from being one of the most opulent into being for a century one of the poorest states in Europe. The brilliant historian of Henry's reign tells us that this transaction was of the nature of a loan. I apprehend, if a burglar or a footpad thinks proper to say that he has borrowed your plate-chest or your purse, that he has not materially modified the transaction by the use of this euphemism. The Stuarts, as I have said, did not go through the form of borrowing—they simply robbed the merchants and the goldsmiths, and through them the widow and the orphan.

The Government of the Revolution borrowed money, but saved public credit. They loaded posterity with debt, but they made good faith traditional in the administration of public affairs. The fact is, responsibility is the guarantee of a public conscience. Governments which are irresponsible, governments, that is to say, which only command a minority of public opinion, are dangerous to the morality of a community, however brief their duration. If they lasted long, they would be fatal to public honour. History is full of examples, near and remote, of this truth. It signifies nothing what the form of government is, whether the faction be dominant in a republic, hold its grip by the machinery of a military despotism, or have an accidental existence under a constitutional monarchy.

At the close of the seventeenth century, the richest county in England, after Middlesex, was Norfolk. York followed, but Lancashire stood only twenty-eighth on the list. There were three and a-half acres to each house in Middlesex, twenty-eight and a-half to each house in Lancashire. At present, the proportion is about two-thirds of an acre in Middlesex, three in Lancashire, and Lancashire stands, by its acreage, second in point of opulence to the metropolitan county. The great centres of industry, where the northern population of these islands is now gathered, were then open moors, wet pastures. The inhabitants, no doubt, led a monotonous life, for they lived in a damp climate, and were contiguous to a melancholy ocean. Lord Dudley had just begun to discover the use of pit coal in smelting Staffordshire iron; but the best bars came from the Sussex forges. The rails round St. Paul's Cathedral were made from the iron of the Wealden. The cloth manufacture was scattered over England. Defoe tells us that its principal localities in the southern counties were Farnham, Alton, Guildford, and Reading, towns known now for other industries, if known at all. Even in those days, however, Newcastle was conspicuous for its glass trade, for the 'London Gazette' contains frequent advertisements of quarries, selling at from 13s. to 10s. the hundred feet.

The 'London Gazette' of the time was published by authority twice or thrice a week. It is a single leaf, of small folio size, printed generally in small type and in double columns. On the one side is foreign intelligence, on the other a short and very succinct account of domestic matters. The last column contains the advertisements. These are of the ordinary character. Notices of library sales; of new books; of picture sales; of quack medicines, Anderson's Scotch pills figuring constantly; rewards offered for runaway negroes, and deserters from Colonel This or That's regiment; of auctions by inch of candle; of patents and inventions. I must not occupy your time with these items. The Government advertisements, printed in italics, head the list, and generally refer to changes in the service of the post, and to contracts for timber. Thus the public is informed that, as the Tunbridge season has commenced, there will be a daily post from London, except on Sundays; again, that a bi-weekly post has been established for Burton-on-Trent, and that a weekly stage coach to Lincoln has been set up for the summer. While the fleet was at the Nore, in the spring of 1692, a mail-bag was also dispatched thither daily. Among stranger advertisements I may mention one of a tradesman in York Buildings, who informs his readers that he is ready to dig up, embalm, and transport from Ireland the bodies of Englishmen of quality who had fallen there; of an Italian lady who sings in the same place; of a book which gives an account of the value of artificial grasses newly introduced to England, such as ray, clover, saintfoin, and lucerne, and offers them for sale at the 'Fleur de Luce,' opposite to the Maypole, in the Strand. And, lastly, in the 'Scotch Mercury' of May 8th, 1692, is the assurance of protection given by the King's Privy Council in Scotland to the Highlanders of Glencoe, the tardy repentance for the atrocious deed of Breadalbane and Stair.

The popular periodical of the time appears to have been a publication like 'Notes and Queries,' or even more like the correspondents' page of the 'Family Herald.' Questions were sent to a bookseller, and after a short interval the printed question and its answer were published. These questions are theological and scientific, or deal with love, courtship, and marriage. At intervals a title-page and index are given, in order that the single sheets may be bound into a volume. Nothing, however, was printed which corresponds to the modern newspaper press.

This is not the place in which to discuss the justification which is commonly alleged for that burden of a public debt which our forefathers put upon us. It is sufficient to say, in the first place, that the heritage was far greater than the burden, and that, even if the statesmen of the age were in error when they strained every nerve to adjust the balance of power, they must, like the statesmen of every age, be judged by their motives. At this time, at least, we may do them the justice to assert that they were seriously alarmed for religion and liberty when they resisted the aggrandisement of Louis, and that it was necessary to break off that dangerous intimacy between the French treasury and leading Englishmen which Louis furthered, and to which Barillon was the go-between. In the next place, there was the plea of necessity. Mr. Hallam alludes to the fact that the customs and excise duties in 1693 had dwindled to less than half their amount before the Revolution. But this author was not at the pains to discover the reason, because, like most historians, he has ignored the economical side of the events which he comments on. During the six years 1686-91 wheat was worth on an average 34*s.* the quarter; during the next six years, the average was 60*s.* 6*d.* The inevitable consequence followed. As the indirect sources of revenue were diminished under the pressure of this dearth, it became necessary to supplement them by direct taxation, in the form of a tax of twenty per cent. on real and personal estate. If the financier of the age burdened posterity with a debt, it must be admitted that he did not spare the existing generation.

In 1691, Montagu was made a Lord of the Treasury and Chancellor of the Exchequer. His first great act was one of singular boldness. For some time past the silver coin had been in a deplorable condition. It was so worn and clipped that a guinea was worth thirty shillings in silver, counted by tale. It was necessary to restore the currency, but on this occasion, as afterwards in 1815, the country gentlemen, with Harley at their head, proposed that the new coins should be issued at the average weight to which the old currency had been reduced. The expedient would have been at once an act of bankruptcy and an act of robbery,—the former because it would have defrauded creditors, the latter because it would have mulcted persons who were in receipt of fixed sums, or of such wages as are not settled by competition. The proposal was rejected.

The other part of Montagu's re-coinage scheme was of more doubtful prudence. He determined that those who deposited their clipped and worn money in the Mint should have new money of full weight in exchange. As a matter of abstract justice, it is clear that the act of coinage, being a service which the Government does for the public, and being a certificate of the fineness contained in the pieces issued, the Exchequer should not be called on to bear the loss of wear, still less losses by fraud. It was plain, too, that having fixed a date at which the coin should be received at the Mint, and having made the date a somewhat distant one, Montagu created two evils—one a sudden abstraction of the currency in circulation, another a strong temptation to still further clip and mutilate the coin. It is certain that the latter temptation was yielded to. The aggregate loss to the nation from this transaction was not less than £3,000,000, nearly £8,500,000 having been brought into the several mints set up in London and elsewhere.

The justification for this lavish act was the discontent which it was believed would be entertained, if the worn and clipped money had been taken by weight. The Government was in a most precarious situation, the expenditure was great, and, as I have observed before, the harvests were unpropitious.

There are those among us who can remember the nuisance which the light sovereigns were some fifteen years ago. It would appear however from a paper lately read in London on the gold circulation of Great Britain, that the people who mulcted the public for light gold, sent the sovereigns back into general circulation and at their full value, immediately after the panic was over.

Part of the difficulty which ensued from the abstraction of the currency during the process of re-coinage, was met by the establishment of the Bank of England. The projector of this was a Scotchman, one Paterson, who afterwards wrecked his fortunes, and those of many others, in the unlucky Darien expedition. The place in which these hapless but venturesome Scots thought proper to found a colony, is one of the most unwholesome under the canopy of heaven. It has its rivals in Massowah, the *teterrima causa* of the late Abyssinian War, and Sierra Leone, the chosen home of fever. These places were at that time unknown to our countrymen. The settlers perished like sheep. It is an illustration of the feeling which persons have entertained as to the responsibility of government, that this failure, due to natural causes, was ascribed for a long time to the jealousy of the English, and that the Scotch made it a condition, at the negotiations which led to the Union, that the loss of the Darien expedition should, in part, be made good. Michael Godfrey, the first governor of the Bank of England, insisted on accompanying William to the siege of Namur, and on needlessly sharing his dangers. He was killed in the trenches.

Those who are familiar with the present operations of the Bank of England, and the influence which the rate of its discount has, not only on the home trade but on the markets of the mercantile world, would smile at the beginnings of the House in Threadneedle Street. In this day, the money market of which the Bank of England is the centre, has greater interest to more men than the rise and fall of empires have. The excommunication of the Stock Exchange is far more terrible, because far more immediately effectual, than the interdict of the pope or the ban of the empire ever were. The price which is paid for the insertion of a stock in the broker's list, is incomparably higher than that which a parvenu pays the Heralds' College for a pedigree and a shield. Unluckily, the certificate is sometimes a cloak for fraud.

In those early days, the Bank had to struggle for existence. It was under the patronage of the Whigs, William being a subscriber of £10,000 stock, as Chamberlain's abortive land bank was under that of the Tories. But as its issues were based on public securities, they were often at a discount, even though they bore a high rate of interest. Droll stories are told by Mr. Francis, the chronicler of the Bank of England, as to the raids which it made on its rivals, and how these rivals organised a run upon it, and how the old Duchess of Marlborough opened her hoards, to avenge herself on her political foes, and sustain the credit of an imperilled establishment. With that woman, revenge was a stronger passion than avarice, though her avarice was proverbial.

In 1696 the credit of the Government had reached its lowest ebb. Tallies on the Exchequer were at from 30 to 60 per cent. discount; Bank notes at 20, and a general bankruptcy seemed imminent. The process of providing the new currency was being carried out, but the want of money was sorely felt. In this crisis, Montagu devised the expedient of Exchequer bills, partly as a floating debt, partly to meet the deficiency of the currency. They bore no interest at first, and were for very small sums. But they were receivable in payment of taxes, and if reissued from the Exchequer, were to carry interest at $5d.$ per cent. per diem, i.e. £7 12s. per annum. The effect of this expedient was almost magical. Credit revived, (perhaps the cessation of the war had something to do with this desirable result,) and from that time forward, the issue of Exchequer bills has been the form in which Government gets its first credit from the House of Commons. Unfortunately, the prevailing immorality of the period led to a dishonest use of these instruments, and several persons were implicated in a fraudulent issue of Exchequer bills. Two representatives convicted of this crime were expelled the House of Commons. The House resolved to punish Duncombe, the Receiver-General of the Excise, and passed a bill levying a fine of £400,000 on this person and his associates, but the Duke of Leeds contrived that the bill should drop in the Lords. Long experience had made the Duke an adept in the art of bribery. Detection could not make him more infamous.

In 1699, Montagu was created Baron Halifax, and was made First Commissioner of the Treasury. He had risen, by dint of sheer industry and keen business faculties, to the post of prime minister, at the age of thirty-eight. Eleven years before, the offer of a living of £150 a year would have determined his career. Now he was a peer, chief minister, had secured certain solid favours from William, and had obtained grants of sinecure offices for himself, his brother, and his nephew. Of course his prosperity procured him some enemies, his vanity and arrogance made him more. But an attempt to impeach him in 1702 failed, after he had lost his office, on the accession of Anne. From that time till 1708, he was one of the junto, his political associates being Somers, Wharton, Orford, and Sunderland. The insolence of the Duchess of Marlborough and the clamour against Sacheverel's impeachment ejected Halifax from power, and set Harley and St. John at the head of affairs. But the amity of St. John and Harley was based on no better foundation than that personal ambition which soon degenerates into sordid rivalry, and despite the efforts of Swift, these two persons came to a rupture, in the last year of Anne's reign. The treasurer was compelled to resign his staff on July 27th, 1714, having been virtually a cipher in the administration for a twelvemonth previously. A cabinet council, which Anne attended, was held the same day. It was at once determined to put the Treasury into the hands of a commission of five. But the ministry could agree to no other name than that of Wyndham, and broke up at two in the morning, without arriving at any decision. The fatigue of this debate was fatal to the Queen. She was seized with apoplexy or gout in the head, and, after a short rally, died on the First of August.

The Queen's sudden or at least unexpected death, broke down the hopes of the Jacobites. Atterbury alone gave bold counsels. He advised Bolingbroke to proclaim the Pretender at once. But the Secretary shrank from the risk. 'There,' said Atterbury, 'goes the best cause for want of a little courage.' The circumstances of the first council, held after the Queen's death, are well known. The Whig leaders insisted on being present, and confounded their opponents; George was proclaimed, and a regency administered public affairs during the King's absence. The Jacobites were furious. They knew the risk before it was a certainty. Lady Masham, whose fortunes departed with her power, railed at Harley on the last day of July with aggravated feminine bitterness, declaring that he had neither sense nor honesty, though when she wrote, Dr. Arbuthnot entertained hopes of the Queen's life, and continued to hope (his judgment being bewildered by his anxieties), up to within a few hours of her death. The council had sent for Radcliffe, then reputed the most sagacious physician in England. Radcliffe declined to come on some pretext or the other, and was charged with having let the Queen die by default. A friend of Radcliffe's moved in the House (for the physician was a member of Parliament), that he should be summoned to his place, and censured for negligence; but the motion was negatived. Radcliffe defended himself, partly by his previous plea, partly by saying that he knew the danger of attending crowned heads, unless under a certificate of indemnity; and then complained characteristically of the ill usage shown him by a friend with whom ' he had drunk many hundred bottles.' In three months the physician died, his end having been, it seems, hastened by the unpopularity which he underwent, and in those days, by the dangers which unpopularity involved.

Bolingbroke was capable of intrigue, but not of action. He could cabal with the backstairs, worry his colleagues, negotiate with the men of letters who were of his party, and debauch as far as possible the House of Commons. Immediately on the Queen's death, he writes to Swift, begging him to remain in England and assist his party; laments the 'banterings of fortune;' states that the Tories are resolved not to be crushed, and that this is enough to prevent such a catastrophe; addresses in that punctilious age Swift as 'dear Jonathan;' and concludes his letter with a characteristic postscript—'The Whigs are a pack of Jacobites, and that shall be the cry in a month.' People talk of the versatility of knaves, but political knavery has few expedients, and the chief trick it uses is that of charging opponents with its own vile purposes. It is no wonder that in a few days Swift's Jacobite correspondents could write to him, that the earth has never produced such monsters as Bolingbroke, Harcourt, and Atterbury; the writer of one letter having been intelligent enough to predict the history of parties so accurately as to say, that 'if the King keeps some Tories in employment, the notion of Whig and Tory will be lost, but that of court and country will arise.' What was really felt at the crisis is seen by the fact, that stocks rose as soon as it became manifest that the law of the Hanoverian succession would be respected.

After the death of Anne, Halifax was again made First Lord of the Treasury, and raised to the dignity of an earl. But he did not long enjoy this later elevation. He was suddenly taken ill on Sunday, May 15th, 1715, and died on the following Thursday.

I cannot allow myself to omit all mention of one act in the public life of Halifax, his successful resistance to the Occasional Conformity Bill of 1702. The object of this measure, which the reactionary Parliament of Anne strove to carry, was to distress the Dissenters. It provided that if any person holding an office of trust, for the occupation of which it was necessary to take the Sacrament, should attend at a Dissenters' meeting-house, he should be disabled from his employment, and be fined a hundred pounds, with five pounds a day additional, as long as, having committed the offence, he remained in office. The management of the bill was put into the hands of Bromley and St. John, the first a violent bigot, the second notorious for his naked scepticism and his naked political apostasy. Halifax managed the conference on the part of the House of Lords, and, for once in the political history of England, had nearly all the Bishops with him, arrayed on the side of good sense and toleration. As the Lords were resolute in their resistance to it, the bill dropped. It was on this occasion that Defoe wrote his 'Shortest Way of Dealing with Dissenters.' He was adjudged to stand in the pillory for two hours, to be imprisoned in Newgate, and to pay a fine of £200. But the London Nonconformists covered the pillory with laurels, pelted their advocate with flowers, and drank to him in silver cups. In 1711, Nottingham contrived to enact this measure of persecution, at the instance of Bolingbroke; but it was repealed in 1719, when Bolingbroke was in exile, and the Whigs were in the ascendant. The Whigs of George the First's days, says Lord Stanhope, were really the Tories of a later date; the Tories Whigs. It is difficult to discover any resemblance beyond such as might appear to the anxious eye of a partisan, when one recollects the persons who supported this atrocious act of persecution.

The accession of Anne had been followed by a political reaction. Fortunately for the principles of the Revolution, Louis the Fourteenth acknowledged the son of James the Second on the death of his father, and in contravention of the treaty of Ryswick. Anne was therefore constrained to defend her crown, and to maintain the principles which her courtiers and she secretly abhorred. Hence the Tories were continually compelled to uphold that which they detested, and to intrigue against their avowed principles. Nothing was so fatal to the hopes of the exiled Jacobites as the ill-considered recognition of James. Had it not been for this event, the reaction might have triumphed. As it was, its only fruit was the nonsense of Dr. Sacheverel, the rival intrigues of the waiting-women, the Duchess of Marlborough and Lady Masham, the victory of the latter, because such a victory was necessarily won by the most supple and compliant, and the defection of Harley and Bolingbroke from the Whig party.

In the autumn of 1710 a clergyman, of English descent, but who was born in Ireland, and who had been presented to a benefice in that island, came to London, ostensibly for the purpose of furthering certain interests of the Irish Church. He had been long known as one of the most active and vigorous political writers of the time, and his assistance had been eagerly courted by both parties. But Swift was unforgiving. The Whigs, shocked, or pretending to be shocked, by the coarse profanity contained in his 'Tale of a Tub,' had withstood his preferment in the Church. Even Wharton, profligate as he was, was justified in saying, 'We must not encourage this fellow; we have not character enough ourselves.' So Swift complained of the coldness of Somers, and the treachery of Halifax, and the bad faith of Berkeley, and the unprincipled character of Wharton, and resolved to desert them. Besides, Swift was shrewd. He saw that the Whig party was discredited; that the reaction consequent on Sacheverel's trial was ruining their fortunes, when he was bent on bettering his own. He came to London, found Godolphin's administration tottering to its fall, and instantly determined on the party to which he should adhere. It was in vain that Halifax entertained him at Hampton Court, and invited him to his country seat. Swift kept up a close friendship with only one of the Whigs. But Addison was popular with everybody. 'If,' says Swift, speaking of the Essayist's election for Malmesbury, 'he had a mind to be chosen king, he could hardly be refused.'

I have spoken of the instruction which the curious may obtain as to the Court of the Restoration by a perusal of Grammont's Memoirs. A similar picture, though drawn by the hand of a greater master, is to be found in Swift's Journal to Stella. The coarse frivolities of fashionable life, the endless intrigues of court lackeys and court waiting-women, the bustle of the Treasurer's levée, the suppers at taverns, the card-parties at Mrs. Manley's, the Mohawks of Covent

Garden, the quarrels and the duels, the gossip and the scandal of the town, are all faithfully described in the plainest possible English, through a series of letters to the young lady whose relations to Swift were then equivocal, and which remain to our days, since history has seldom leisure for private scandal, eminently mysterious.

The Queen, who was to be wheedled into whatever policy seemed most convenient for the ambition of her ministers, made no very considerable figure in the drama. She had merely exchanged the tutelage of Sarah Duchess of Marlborough for that of Abigail Lady Masham. Other monarchs have been governed by confessors: Anne shaped her policy by the whims of her favourite waiting-woman. Swift saw her when he was using his pen on behalf of her ministers, as Johnson saw her in his childhood, when she touched him for the King's evil—a fat, gouty, lethargic woman, in black velvet and diamonds.

The most mysterious man of that time was Harley, the Prime Minister. Before he reached this dignity, he had been Speaker of the House of Commons. Bred a Dissenter, he became the chief of the High Tory party. Introduced into the Cabinet in 1704, as a Whig, and made Secretary of State, he carried with him St. John, another Whig, as Secretary at War. Both intrigued against Godolphin and Marlborough, through the assistance of Mrs. Masham, and were forced to retire from office in 1708; for the statesman and the soldier threatened to resign their places unless these cabals were repudiated. But Harley after his dismissal, intrigued again through the same channel, and ultimately succeeded in ejecting Godolphin, and occupying his office. He held this place to within a few days of the Queen's death. Almost every man in England, who thought on the matter, believed that the sole object which Harley had before him was the restoration of the Stuarts. Bolingbroke thought so, and committed himself finally, and for himself fatally, to the project. But George succeeded at Anne's death quietly, though absent from England; nor, when the conduct of the ministers was impeached after the accession of the Hanoverian line, was Harley found to have played false to any but those who had believed in his reputed opinions. Even these people had no other proof than the strength of their own presumption. Harley never committed himself. To a moral certainty he would have been exposed, had he done any overt act of political apostasy; for the Whigs were not likely to be tender of public reputations after the Scotch rising of 1715.

Beyond doubt, Harley had consummate art in the most difficult and delicate of all finesse, the management of the House of Commons. He quarrelled with no man, had a kind word for everybody. 'Don't come to my levée,' he said to Swift, 'I have no friends there.' He dropped in to parties, and chatted familiarly with every one he met. He rallied his acquaintances as though they had been friends. His kindness of manner to his reputed friends knew no bounds. He called Swift 'Presto,' and Swift was as proud of the name as if it had been a peerage. Swift, the most jealous, vain, exacting of men, never suspected that Harley used him as a mere political tool. Harley had no policy, and was therefore able to say that any expedient was his original purpose. He ridiculed Sacheverel, the Murphy of the day, and gave him secret support. He was on good terms with the Jacobites, but he was also on good terms with the House of Hanover. The former believed that he would restore 'the King,' the latter that he would save the Act of Succession. It was only when he disappointed the former that Bolingbroke, a ruined political gamester, uttered, in his letter to Wyndham, that savage judgment on him, 'that he had a weak spirit and a wicked soul.' And when he slunk out of office, his enemies rejoiced over his fall, and joined the Whigs in their second act of folly. The first was the prosecution of Sacheverel, the other was the impeachment of Harley. They did not see that Harley was an accomplished dissembler, who had one object before him, that of being Prime Minister. He was satisfied with his success when he reached his dignity, and he enjoyed it for four years. People believed that he was a sphinx—a great mystery; but he was really a man with much tact, infinite good temper, no principles, a sincere belief in himself, and a total indifference as to the means by which he might rise to eminence. He would, I make no doubt, have preferred remaining a Dissenter and a Whig; against his will, and in his own interest, he became a Tory, and was thought to be a Jacobite. If Bolingbroke, instead of being a courtier, an intriguer, and a freethinker, had been a country gentleman of our day, he would have wished his Leader to have been in heaven, or in some other place, at the great crisis of 1714.

The most noteworthy fact in the political history of that epoch which lies between the accession of William and the death of Anne, was the public employment of men who had no recommendation beside their capacity. Such men were, for example, Prior, Addison, Steele, Tickell. Swift himself might have been Secretary to the Embassy at Vienna, and this at a most critical period. The Bishop of Bristol negotiated the peace of Utrecht. The scene changed when Walpole came into power, and inaugurated a new system of government. This minister ruled the country party by pensions and peerages, by honours and hard cash, by the simplest, and, for a time, the cheapest expedients. He had learnt his lesson in Opposition; and in those days, the Opposition was not only hungry, but desperate, and, for its personal ends, preternaturally acute.

Through the epoch which I have spoken of, the public life of Halifax lasted. He was the first finance minister that England had. He understood the conditions of public credit, and he had, for his time, a clear comprehension of the machinery which is needed for mercantile prosperity. I cannot say that, had he lived long enough, he would have saved England from the wild frenzy which culminated in the South Sea Scheme. Within our own experience, a greater financier than Montagu was at the head of affairs when Parliament sanctioned the mad speculations of the great railway bubble; when projects were legalised, the completion of which would have required more than the annual earnings of capital and labour to effect them; when Capel Court renewed the memories of 'Change Alley, and the Craggses and Aislabies were reproduced too numerously for reprobation and punishment.

The commencement of responsible government was the commencement of the science of finance. But this science is yet only in its infancy. The problem is twofold,—how to combine efficiency with economy in the public service; how to adjust public burdens so that taxation shall be equitable. But these are only the most obvious of those numerous economical questions, the solution of which is of pressing importance, which grow in urgency as they are delayed, and which have been delayed, only in deference to clamorous interests.

SIR ROBERT WALPOLE,

EARL OF ORFORD.

SIR ROBERT WALPOLE,

EARL OF ORFORD.

THE antiquarian who gives his attention to the beginnings of constitutional history in England, finds the germ of that theory of government which surrounds the monarch with ministerial advisers, in the peremptory and despotic administration of Henry the Eighth. This prince, who more than any other English king ruled by sheer force of will, appears to have been the author of a system which has ultimately destroyed the power which it was intended to assist, usurped the functions which it was intended to strengthen. As the Merovingian kings appointed their Mayors of the Palace, and the descendants of Charles the Great trusted to the Counts of Paris, only to find masters and successors in their ministers and political servants, so the House of Tudor invented the machinery which, professing to maintain all the forms of monarchical institutions, has made this country to all intents and purposes a republic, the chief magistrates of which are elected by the popular branch of the Legislature, and are controlled by an opposition which is only a little more informal than the organisation which it criticises, attacks, or condemns. The circumstances which have developed the limited monarchy of the United Kingdom are wholly fortuitous, if indeed that is accidental which has not only not been foreseen, but which has originated by gradual progression from a system which was intended to counteract the very consequences which have ensued from it.

The government of a country by a board of administrators, who are in theory heads of official departments, and whose councils and policy originate in a conclave which has no legal existence, who are called into being by the approval of Parliament, and who are extinguished by its disapproval, is almost peculiar to ourselves. In almost every country but our own the will of the chief magistrate counts for something. In the most popular or democratic governments it counts for a great deal. We have lately witnessed a singularly unseemly controversy, carried on between the chief of the American Republic and the Houses of Parliament in the American Union. The legislative and executive functions have been in constant collision, and the civilised world has been amused or scandalised, while the public policy of the great Commonwealth of North America has been checked by a deadlock. Between this political system and the Cæsarism which identifies the will of the monarch with the life of the State, there are numerous varieties of personal government more or less autocratic. But there are no institutions precisely like our own, in which the ministers of government are constituted or displaced by a simple and energetic machinery, that by which the popular Council of the Nation grants its confidence to an administration, or withdraws its countenance from it. It is a century and a-half since the Crown has put its veto on a measure sanctioned by both Houses; it is nearly as long a time since the Crown has pursued an independent policy, that is, has supported or resisted measures which have obtained a concurrent majority in the opinion of both Houses. The early princes of the Hanoverian House were willing enough to be despotic, and sometimes succeeded in cajoling one of the Estates into supporting their prejudices or convictions, but they have never been able to take a wholly independent line of action by the aid of their ministers.

This singular adjustment of political forces has been developed from a simple formula. The Crown is irresponsible, but its advisers are under a perpetual responsibility. In early times this responsibility was secured by the right of impeachment, which the Legislature has asserted for five hundred years. Later, the same result has been attained by the milder method of a vote of no confidence, an act of political ostracism under which an administration is as effectually constrained to abdicate as Continental monárchs have been by revolutions. Nor could the most resolute prince resist. He is not indeed chargeable, according to the respectful language of our constitution, with the errors or crimes of his advisers. But until he appoints or accepts others, who possess the confidence denied to their predecessors, the whole mechanism of administration is arrested or suspended. These facts are indeed familiar enough to us all, but they represent a political system which is not merely singular but unique.

It is impossible to define in an unwritten or traditional constitution, and nearly as impossible in a constitution which is precisely defined, what are the relative functions of legislative and executive forces. In this country we have given the fullest power to the latter, but have made those who wield the forces absolutely dependent on the former. Had no such agencies interposed between the ruler and the subject, the limitation of either's rights would have been the material for a perpetual and ever-varied conflict. The struggle would have been provoked by the personal will, the abilities, the impulses, even by the physical constitution of the former, as these vary in different individuals, or in the same individual. Parliaments too, like monarchs, have their idiosyncrasies, and there would be in the struggle between these rivals, a perpetual ebb and flow of prerogative and liberty, of executive authority and legislative control. Such a political system did indeed characterise our parliamentary history for many a century. The Legislature was variably strong and weak from the days of the first Edwards to the Revolution, sometimes assuming great powers, as in the times of Richard the Second and Charles the First, sometimes sinking almost to the level which was reached by the French Parliaments of the ancient monarchy, as in the days of Henry the Eighth and Charles the Second.

The theory of ministerial responsibility, guaranteed as it was in very early days by the right of parliamentary impeachment, was, like many analogous institutions, of very slow growth. Familiar as the process is, it is really a remarkable political abstraction, as abstruse as some of those metaphysical paradoxes which exercised the ingenuity of the schoolmen. It affirms the form of monarchical institutions, and, without making an election, confers the executive powers of the State on the elected head of a legislative republic. No publicist, I may venture to affirm, would have ever dreamed of developing so peculiar, and at first sight so contradictory and illogical a process of force and check, from any theory of government. And, for the same reason, no such system could have suddenly sprung up. It must have been produced slowly, though it may perhaps be imitated without difficulty by other political communities. Had it been fully developed at the epoch of the American War of Independence, it is probable that Washington and his associates would have adopted its provisions. The founders of the American republic had two difficulties before them of no common magnitude. The first of these was how they could secure the municipal independence of the several states comprising the Union, and grant at the same time a respectable autonomy to the federal councils.

The second was the harmony between the executive and legislative functions of the president and these councils. So great was the former difficulty, that much diplomacy and not a little deceit, if indeed the latter can be distinguished from the former, was employed by Franklin in order to effect the union, a union which, as we all know, was bound by a very precarious tie. The latter is even now unsolved, though the solution would have been easier had the ministers of the President been absolutely responsible to Congress and the Senate, instead of being responsible to those powers for a crisis only, that is, at the moment of their appointment.

One of the commonest errors into which superficial critics of political events fall, is that of interpreting past forces by the light of present experience. People talk and write of the administration of Edward the Third's days, as though they were discussing the social phenomena of a time in which the forces of government had each its definition, place, and function. But at that time, and for many a century afterwards, each force in the social machine was seeking to secure itself and to assert further powers, and this at the expense of personal government, that is, by revolution. We speak of revolution with alarm. But, in fact, revolutions are matters of degree, varying not in kind but in intensity, between the simple but organic changes which acquire the force of law and abiding precedent, and earthquakes which frequently level buildings only that they may be built up again in the same form but with greater solidity. The English revolution of 1688 was to outward appearance a mere change of dynasty, accompanied by a few constitutional guarantees, the force of which was for a long time imperfectly understood, the spirit of which was for a longer time only imperfectly appreciated. But it was a real and great advance. The French revolution of a century later shook the political world to its centre. It affected to wholly ignore the past, except in its allusions to republican Greece and Rome. It has left a few superficial marks on French society. It has effected an equality before the law. It has divided the estate of a deceased ancestor equally, or almost equally, among his children or descendants. But it has not given a single guarantee to human liberty, has not warranted its assertions, has not justified itself. At the present moment, France is reproducing the social system of Louis Quatorze, only in a coarser shape, with all the extravagance, waste, licentiousness, irritable vanity, aggressiveness, bounce, superficial orthodoxy, hard scepticism, heartlessness, intellectual brilliancy, intellectual depravity, which characterised that epoch. It is not easy to say what humanity has gained by the French revolution. It would be a long story to recount what it has lost by that upheaval.

The social history of this time is to be gathered from sources like Hervey's Memoirs, Horace Walpole's Letters to Sir Horace Mann, and similar materials—the works of men who, having no motive to praise or blame, are valuable authorities in proportion to their opportunities for learning, and capacity for interpreting the facts to which they witness. Similarly a composition of Hogarth's gives us a clear conception of the outer life of London, such as those of the 'Election,' the 'March to Finchley,' 'Gin Alley,' and 'Beer Lane.' How strange that the art of the painter has produced one Hogarth only, has never, except in this case, developed pictorial comedy!

Between June 11, 1727, and October 25, 1760, the foremost personage in this country was a little fussy man, who talked incessantly and fluently, though with a strong foreign accent, was snappish beyond measure to those he liked the best or respected the most, was plentiful in coarse abuse on the smallest provocation, or no provocation at all, had a fairly strong memory of injuries, and none whatever of benefits or services. He is reported to have loved one person, his mother, the unhappy Sophia Dorothea, though the best proof that this feeling was not derived from his hatred to his father lay in the fact that immediately on his accession he set up his mother's picture in his cabinet. He is reported to have respected one person, and that was his wife. He hated his eldest son with the greatest bitterness, much more bitterly than his father had hated him. It may be doubted whether he rejoiced more at his father's death than he did at his son's.

George the Second had a marvellous faculty for shedding copious tears on the shortest notice and the most trivial occasions. When his eldest daughter married the Prince of Orange, he gave her, says Hervey, a thousand kisses, a shower of tears, but not a single guinea. When Walpole pressed his Excise scheme in the House of Commons, and nearly ruined himself in the attempt, George used to blurt out, with flushed cheeks and gushing eyes, 'He is a brave fellow; he has more spirit than any man I know.' He wept incessantly during the Queen's last illness, though he was at the time arranging the journey of that Madame Walmoden whom the heralds know as the Countess of Yarmouth. He wept still more abundantly when his minister retired from his councils. But there was always a mixture of brutality in his tenderest acts and words.

When Walpole's administration was in the greatest peril, because it was believed that the King had perished in the storms of December 1736, the great minister spoke of the King as his 'sweet master,' and was profoundly anxious for his safety. But the same minister two years before had said of George, that 'to talk to him of compassion, consideration for past services, charity, and bounty, was to make use of words which bore no meaning to him.' His avarice was enormous. The beginnings of his quarrel with his worthless son were over money matters. He could not endure to increase Frederic's income out of his civil list to the amount which he had received himself. He loved his army more than anything else, and insisted that he should manage it himself.

But he kept important places in the service vacant for very niggardliness, not because it would have cost him anything to fill them up, but from sheer dislike to giving anything away. He crippled Walpole by refusing to allow him the means of corrupting the House of Commons through the Horse Guards. A generation or two later, and this portion of the prerogative was conceded to the Ministry.

He had, it seems, one conversational gift. He was able (and I presume it is easier for kings to do this than for subjects) to turn away any topic which displeased him. He also invented the cut direct, for he had the trick of looking at the place in which his son stood as though no one were there. To his family he was a bore of the first water. He entertained the Queen with a minute description of his Hanoverian picnics with Madame Walmoden. When he was away, he filled reams of paper with similar details, which were regularly posted to his wife. Caroline sat during these recitals sometimes yawning, sometimes smiling, always knotting. She regularly and as fully answered his letters. His daughters were less patient, and when he prosed over the old story of his courage, and fearlessness, and presence of mind, they pretended to be asleep. Lord Hervey affects to be shocked at their duplicity. The daughters would have been more undutiful still, had they not hated and feared their brother too heartily to resent anything from their father.

Queen Caroline was her husband's good genius.

Her father-in-law loathed her, and invariably spoke of her as a she-devil. She simply lived for the King. It is possible that she loved him; but she certainly made the furtherance of his interests, and the study of his caprices, and even the satisfaction of his peculiar pleasures, the entire business of her existence. She either did not feel, or she perfectly dissimulated any resentment at his conduct. She condescended with the strangest alacrity to the strangest compliances, not indeed passively, but actively, not with him alone, but in concert with Walpole for him. She guided him in everything, where guidance was possible; but always affected to defer to his opinion. It is possible that he was taken in by an affectation of profound and perpetual humility. It is said that she loved power. But she does not appear to have ever willingly exercised any direct influence in public affairs, and she certainly never wished her husband to prolong his Hanoverian visits. She was regent during the King's lengthiest absence, perhaps necessarily, but she knew well enough that her occupation of this office only embittered her son towards her. Nor was her office a sinecure during the crisis of Madame Walmoden's fascinations. There was rioting in the West against the corn-laws; rioting in Spitalfields against the Irish immigrants; rioting in Scotland against civil authority, when the Edinburgh mob broke into the Tolbooth, and hanged Porteous in the Grass-market.

The Queen was as little fastidious in her language as she was sensitive on topics about which queens are, we may suppose, like other women. She jested with Hervey, with Walpole, with Stair, with Kinski, in the broadest and plainest fashion. She was always alert, sprightly, and keen. She was, when she spoke of men and things, the impersonation of good sense. 'The triple alliance,' she said, 'between Spain, France, and Sardinia, puts me in mind of the South-Sea scheme, which the parties concerned in entered into, not without knowing the cheat, but hoping to make advantage of it, everybody designing when he had made his fortune, to be the first in scrambling out of it, and each thinking himself wise enough to be able to leave his fellow-adventurers in the lurch.' The parallel of a commercial bubble and a diplomatic alliance entered into for military purposes, is close and exact. History reproduces itself. The triple alliance of 1853, as far as two of the high contracting parties were concerned, was of a piece with that to which the Queen alluded when she compared this diplomatic intrigue to a vast commercial fraud. The third part of the parallel fails only, because it represents a minister instead of a monarch.

It was part of the Queen's conjugal duty to hate her son. If she did not really hate him, her dissimulation was astonishing. Her daughter Caroline was at one with her mother. 'No one would credit,' says Hervey, 'unless he heard, the names they called him, the character they gave him, the curses they lavished on him, and the fervour with which they prayed every day for his death.' I presume that there never was any other mother who said of her son, that 'he was the greatest ass, the greatest liar, the greatest canaille, and the greatest beast in the world, and that she heartily wished he was out of it.' The daughter had another reason, for when she dined with her brother, he insisted that she should sit on a stool, and be served with diminished state. It is, however, difficult to arrive at the reasons for this unnatural disgust. The bitterness and the provocations seem more like the mad unreasoning rage which is sometimes entertained by monks and nuns against each other, when they are constrained to be perpetually together.

The Queen sacrificed her health, and finally her life, to her husband. She had been sorely tried by her alarm for the King's safety in the preceding winter, and had undergone fresh anxiety when Pulteney, as leader of the opposition, had tried to get an increase of the Prince's allowance. After strenuous efforts, the proposal was defeated by 230 votes to 204. 'The victory was supposed,' said Walpole, 'to have cost a great deal of money. It really was settled,' he continued, 'by a bribe of some £400 or £500, given to two men.' These circumstances aggravated the disease under which she suffered, and which she had concealed from every one but Lady Sundon. Something may be said, too, for the comparative unskilfulness of the surgeons at that time. The secret was valuable, however, to the lady in waiting. So elated was this personage with the interest which this confidence seemed to give her, that she actually proposed to Walpole that they should join hands, and govern the nation between them. Walpole answered, that he preferred the rule of the King and Queen, but added that, if she contrived to effect such an alliance with any other statesman, he hoped that he might reckon on her countenance. The Queen died, and Pope, that 'mens curva in corpore curvo,' as Atterbury described him, continued, as might have been anticipated, to lampoon her in her grave, in an epigram which has no parallel for coarse spite. She cared little for lampoons in her life. She had the good sense to know that monarchs are always calumniated, and that half the wit and all the malignity of a calumny are neutralised by indifference. The King's sorrow for his wife's death gave him a popularity which he never enjoyed before. As long as he could, too, he followed her dying advice. She summoned Walpole to her deathbed, and said, 'I have nothing to tell you, but to recommend the King, my children, and the kingdom to your care.' She loved one of her sons as much as she hated the other. That son was William, whose reputation was made at Culloden, and lost at Closterseven.

Aristotle tells a droll story of a family in Greece, in which a son was dragging his father to the door of their house, and was about to turn him out, when the father remonstrated, and said, 'Up to the door it is fair enough, for I dragged my father to this point, and then stopped;' and adds that the apology for the scandal was to be found in the fact that such acts of violence were characteristic of the family. A similar explanation was given in the last century of the quarrels between father and son in the Hanoverian dynasty. George the First and his son were estranged; George the Second and his son abandoned all decency in their quarrel. It is not clear that a similar feud arose in the next family, but it is certain that the son gave occasion enough for such a broil. The explanation is more natural when one reflects on the fact that the causes of difference between George the Second and the Prince were so utterly frivolous. The Prince wanted a larger allowance, and was annoyed at not being made regent in his father's absence; and committed his crowning offence by bringing the Princess, just before his eldest daughter's birth, to London against the King's express direction. A similarly trivial circumstance precipitated matters between George the First and his son. The King had appointed the Duke of Newcastle godfather to his grandson, the unlucky Frederic, and Prince George insulted the Duke after the ceremony was over.

It is manifest that Frederic, though his character has generally been drawn by those who sided with the King, was profuse, vain, arrogant, and uncertain. He might have inherited all these vices but the first from his father. The enmity which sprung up between them might have made him headstrong and obstinate. But it is not necessary to derive such traits from hereditary tendencies. The youth of Edward the Second and of Henry the Fifth were equally marked by wilfulness and disobedience.

I have already stated that a century ago the English monarchs had many opportunities for making their will felt in the conduct of public affairs. When kings are absolute, the eldest son is but the principal subject, and cannot intrigue, except cautiously and secretly. But when the monarch's will is controlled by constitutional forms—but especially when he still exercises a real influence in the choice of his ministers—the opposition naturally seeks its head in the Crown Prince. The heir of the Prussian monarchy has always sided with the liberal party, the King with the despotic. Thus Frederic associated himself with the Patriots, his grandson with Fox's adherents. Had Frederic lived to succeed his father, he would as assuredly have allied himself with the Whigs of Walpole's school as his son accepted the services of Pelham, and as his grandson, when he came to the regency, employed Castlereagh and Sidmouth. Deeply as the Prince of Wales hated Walpole, passionately as he longed for his downfal, eagerly as he furthered his impeachment in 1732, he would, I feel persuaded, have been reconciled to him by the force of circumstances in the spring of 1737, had George the Second perished in the storm of the previous December. But though the fact that the position of the Prince of Wales naturally made him the rallying-point of the opposition, it is not marvellous that he was suspected, and, considering the temper of the King, finally hated by his father.

In these days, the strength of the House of Lords consisted in the control which its members exercised over the nomination boroughs. It was to his enormous patronage in these representative shams that the silly and perfidious Duke of Newcastle owed his prolonged power. It is almost unnecessary to say, that the political influence of an hereditary chamber must, under a popular and responsible Government, be secured by indirect means. When Walpole, then Earl of Orford, met his ancient rival, Pulteney, the new Earl of Bath, on the floor of the House of Lords, he said, 'Here we are, my lord, the two most insignificant fellows in the kingdom.' But a century ago, such words could not have been used, even in jest, of Newcastle, Devonshire, and Marlborough.

The House of Commons was, as far as most of the boroughs were concerned, filled with nominees. The Scotch members from both boroughs and counties were of the same character, though, strangely enough, Scotland sometimes cast a vote in favour of public liberty. When in 1718, Lord Stanhope, to his great honour, proposed the repeal of the Occasional Conformity Act, and was opposed by the Tories, and nearly the whole bench of Bishops, carrying his measure by eighty-six votes to sixty-eight, and when the measure was passed in the Lower House, by 243 votes to 202, it is noteworthy that thirty-four Scotch members out of thirty-seven voted for the repeal.

With such people from such boroughs, popular representation would have been a total farce, but for the county electors. The strength of the nation, the guarantees of civil liberty, lay in the freeholders and in a few large towns. In those days, there were yeomen tilling their own lands with a conscious and sturdy independence. The latifundia of our time had hardly begun to exist, and the great proprietors were obliged to defer to the wishes and political opinions of these resolute freeholders, if they were at all ambitious of representing counties in Parliament. Nor can it be doubted that the influence of the county electors was indirectly felt by the proprietors of the nomination boroughs. A century and a half ago, even a Duke of Newcastle could not have ventured on angrily inquiring whether he had not a right to do what he would with his own, even though the Duke were such a man as he was of whom Hervey said; that 'he and Chancellor King both spoke plentifully, and both equally unintelligibly—the latter from having lost his understanding, the former from never having had any.' How rapid has been, even in recent days, the elimination of these freeholders, is seen in the fact, that the number of such electors in the county of Berkshire was greater before the Act of 1832 than that of all the electors prior to the reform of 1867.

It was, I repeat, in the counties and some large boroughs that political feeling was kept alive. It was in these that the most vehement contests of parties were witnessed. The impoverishment of many an ancient family, the embarrassment of more, can be traced back to these conflicts. The Oxfordshire election of 1754 was famous for generations. So was that of Appleby, between Lowther and Lord Thanet, for it cost £55,000. In the year before Walpole's fall there was a similar contest for Westminster, where every effort was made to return candidates unfavourable to the ministry. The effort was successful. 'We should have carried the Westminster election,' said Lord Chesterfield, 'if we had set up two broomsticks.' 'So I see,' said Lord Lovel. The poll was carried on till the electors were exhausted, or one of the candidates retired. Bribery, notwithstanding the Act of 1729, flourished and struck deep root.

Petitions and disputed returns were investigated by a committee of the whole House. It is almost unnecessary to say, that in that age, when factions strove bitterly for the mastery, fairness was the last thing thought of. The most outrageous decisions were arrived at. The scandal of these proceedings was monstrous. In one case, the House voted that forty was more than ninety. In another, they cut off the votes of seven towns and some thousands of voters. The decision as to whether the electoral franchise was conferred on the corporation, the freemen, or the scot-and-lot voters, was affirmed or rescinded on party grounds. Hervey, in the most natural way, complains of this injustice, and asserts that the House thought nothing of robbing a man of his seat, after he had paid several thousand pounds to gain it; and moralizes, as we might moralize from other and later instances, 'that when shame is divided among five hundred men, the portion of each individual is so small, that it hurts their pride as little as it disconcerts their countenances.' Those advocates of that privilege of Parliament which consists in controlling elections, examining disputed returns, and deciding on the qualification of candidates, have probably forgotten the scandals which preceded the passing of Grenville's Act. Perhaps they do not even recollect how uncertain were the principles which guided the smaller committees of our own day.

Walpole fell in consequence of an adverse vote given by one of these election committees in 1742; the body of Patroclus, round which the Achæans and Trojans waged battle, being the borough of Chippenham. To any feeling besides the pedantic attachment to precedent, nothing could be more ludicrous than the fact that a ministry succumbed to a verdict on a disputed claim to a seat in the House; a verdict—the word had ceased to have any etymological meaning—which should have been determined by justice and not by party passion.

Another strange rule which the House of Commons at that time maintained with the greatest severity, was that of enforcing secrecy about its proceedings. The regulation was once a guarantee of freedom of speech against regal despotism. It was well enough in the days of the five members, when kings turned eavesdroppers by themselves or by deputy; but it was a mere blind to corruption at a time when Parliament was all-powerful. In consequence, the kings of the limited monarchy learned that coercion, except when the members held place or pension, was impracticable or clumsy, and Walpole, following the precedent of Louis the Fourteenth in dealing with Charles the Second's long parliament, adopted bribery in place of intimidation. He saw that force is not so powerful as persuasion, just as we have at last understood, though slowly and imperfectly, that the real remedy for treason is to make it ridiculous, the real remedy for disaffection is to make a people well affected.

Those burgesses and knights of the shire who gathered under the roof of old St. Stephen's, clad in the costume which the Court has crystallized up to our time, bewigged, and girt with swords, carried on the strife of selfish faction under the guise of parliamentary forms. One of two faculties was needed for any man who aspired to be a party leader. He must be skilful with his weapon, or quick with his tongue. At no time, I believe, has wit been more keen, repartee more smart. There was no seriousness, no earnest conviction abroad, but infinite cleverness. The best poet, almost the only poet, was Pope, and he elaborated social satire more exquisitely than any writer before or since. But there is not a germ of conscientiousness in all his poetry. The letters, the memoirs, the essays of the time, sparkle with humour, are strewn with felicitous retorts; but they contain no beliefs. The latest and the greatest of these wits was Wilkes, whose pungent and lively sallies are even yet remembered.

At the commencement of George the Second's reign there were four parties in the House of Commons. There were a few acknowledged Jacobites, of whom the leader was Shippen. These men were on the whole dispirited and indifferent. There were the Hanover Tories, the friends of the new settlement, but still more the allies of the clerical party. Sir Thomas Hanmer might be said to lead them. There were Whigs out of place, whose chief was Pulteney, and who called themselves patriots; and Whigs in place, who were called courtiers, and who were under the guidance of Walpole.

Robert Walpole was the second son of a Norfolk squire, who sat for King's Lynn up to the beginning of the eighteenth century, and was a steady Whig. The old man, said his grandson Horace, left among his memoranda an account of his expenses in London during a session of three months and ten days. They amounted to £64 7s. 5d., a sum, says the virtuoso, which we should think nothing of giving for a fan or a toy. Among the items of this expenditure is 'five shillings for Bob.'

This 'Bob' was the Minister. The policy of Elizabeth was aided for nearly forty years by William Cecil, but the Queen was rather counselled than guided by her astute secretary. The younger Pitt ruled for nearly twenty years; Lord Liverpool for fifteen. But the reigns of Prime Ministers since the Revolution have, on the average, been shorter than those of Popes. Walpole's was the longest, for he governed the three kingdoms uninterruptedly for twenty-one years.

He was born on August 26, 1676. Originally intended for the Church, as being the second son, he was sent, as his younger brother Horace was, to Eton, and King's College, Cambridge. The death of his elder brother made him heir to an estate of £2,000 a-year, and he was returned to Parliament in 1700 for Castle Rising, and soon after for the borough which his father represented, King's Lynn, and for which he sat till he took his peerage. He was soon employed, for he was appointed Secretary at War in the room of St. John in 1708, and was made Treasurer of the Navy in 1710, when he acted as manager of Sacheverell's impeachment. On Harley's accession to power he was expelled the House on a charge of corruption, and imprisoned in the Tower for seven months. On the accession of George he was made Paymaster, and soon afterwards First Lord of the Treasury and Chancellor of the Exchequer. Two years later he was turned out of office by Sunderland, but was again made Paymaster in 1720. In the next year Sunderland resigned, and Walpole again became Prime Minister. He held office till Feb. 1742, when he resigned and was raised to the peerage. He still, however, though officially in retirement, advised the King, and thwarted his enemies. He died three years after his resignation, on March 18, in the sixty-ninth year of his age.

The management of public affairs during the six years of George the First's reign, in which Walpole was Prime Minister, was easy. Fortunately for him, the South Sea bubble had been blown during Sunderland's administration. Walpole had grown rich by judicious speculation, and by more judicious realization during the mania, for he sold his stock at £1,000 the share. He now assumed office with the object of extricating the nation from the embarrassments into which it had fallen in consequence of the wild schemes upon which so many had embarked and wrecked their fortunes. Simultaneously with Walpole's accession to power Atterbury's plot had been detected and crushed, the bishops being foremost in the attack on their restless and haughty brother. The King, to be sure, was rapacious and selfish, accustomed to look on England as an appanage to Hanover, and as fond of his electoral dominions as he hated his wife and son. Walpole retained his power by small compliances, and of course supported the King against the Prince. His political fortunes seemed to be ruined by George the First's death. That King's successor had ransacked a very copious vocabulary of abuse, in order to stigmatise the minister and his associates. Rogue and rascal, scoundrel and fool, were his commonest utterances when Robert Walpole's name was mentioned. Similarly, he called Horace Walpole a dirty buffoon, Newcastle an impertinent fool,—the most just, by the way, of these contumelious descriptions,—and Townsend, Walpole's brother-in-law, a choleric blockhead, with nearly equal justice. Nor was Walpole more courteous. He had constantly spoken contemptuously of the Prince, and had nicknamed Caroline in a way which a less prudent and more sensitive woman would have held unpardonable, and would never have pardoned.

Walpole bowed meekly to the coming storm. The King sent for Sir Spencer Compton, and everybody hastened to pay his court to the new favourite. Sir Spencer, with a simplicity which seems incredible, requested Walpole to write the King's speech, and the ex-minister agreed to do so with the utmost humility and complaisance. It is superfluous to say that he composed it with the greatest care; and that he made no secret of his authorship. It was impossible that such a farce could be carried out. The King, taking counsel with his wife in reality, though affecting, as he always did, to act on his own judgment, said that the writer of the speech must be the minister; and the Queen sent a message to Walpole, informing him, in her characteristic way, that his coarse allusion to her personal appearance had been remembered, to be forgiven. After Walpole's disgrace, Sir Spencer Compton was allowed to succeed him, under the name of Lord Wilmington.

At first, Walpole was associated with his brother-in-law, Townsend. But they soon disagreed, and the rupture was total after the death of Walpole's sister, Townsend's wife. 'As long,' said the minister, 'as the firm was Townsend and Walpole all went well, but as soon as it came to be Walpole and Townsend all went ill.' Lord Hervey gives another reason for the difference. Before Walpole betook himself to the adornment of Houghton, Raynham was the handsomest seat in Norfolk, then the richest county in England. Townsend's vanity was deeply wounded when the splendour of his house was eclipsed by that of his brother-in-law. To be sure, Hervey had no liking for him, describing him, in a manner which reminds us of Swift, 'as more tenacious of his opinion than of his word, for the one he never gave up, the other he seldom kept; as blunt without being severe, and false without being artful.' He further adds (and here we may recognise a comment of Walpole), 'that he affected great strokes in politics, which a wise minister should be incapable of concerting without the utmost necessity.'

After Townsend's dismissal, Walpole reigned alone, if, indeed, he could be said to exercise sole functions while Newcastle was tied to him. Long before he was betrayed by this person, of whom he justly said that his name was perfidy, he knew how dangerous was the association. But Newcastle was the largest proprietor of rotten boroughs in the kingdom, and, fool and knave as he was, he had wit enough to guess at his own importance, and knavery enough to make his market. Walpole's chief business lay in managing the King, the Queen, the Church, the House of Commons, and perhaps the people.

I have already said, that before his accession George hated Walpole. But there are hatreds and hatreds, equal in fervency while they last, but different in duration. The King hated Walpole because he had served his father well. But one George was gone, and another George was in possession. Then came before the man in possession the clear vision of Walpole's consummate usefulness. The vision was made clearer by the sagacious hints of the Queen. It became clear as noonday when Walpole contrived to add £115,000 to the civil list; for there was one thing which the King loved more than Hanover, and Queen, and children, and Lady Suffolk, and Madame D'Elitz, the mistress to three generations of the House of Hanover, and sister to Lady Chesterfield, and the Walmoden — and that was money. Besides, Walpole was sincerely determined to support the Hanoverian succession. He constantly insisted to George that the final settlement of his House on the throne would be fought out in England. It was clear that a man who was so prescient, would be also most capable of meeting the mischief whenever it should come. Hence he was able to check one of the King's ruling passions, a longing to engage in war; for George was certainly brave, though given to gasconade, and would have greedily entered into a succession of campaigns, if he could only chastise the King of Prussia, his brother-in-law, whom he hated with one of those enduring hatreds which I have referred to. And Walpole was in the right. Three years and a half after his fall, six months after his death, came the march to Derby, and the packing up of the property at Hampton and St. James's, and the peril of the Protestant succession—a peril which it seems was met by the facts, that the young Pretender was ill-advised or dishonest enough to proclaim dubiously about keeping faith with the public creditor, and was scrupulous enough to persevere in a religion which the English nation hated and feared. The House of Stuart is the last royal stock which has ever allowed its religious convictions to be a bar to preferment. In these days, ruling families are always ready with an 'eirenicon;' are conveniently versatile, whenever political exigencies summon them to embrace an alternative of creeds.

The Queen was predisposed in favour of the minister. She knew his value to herself and her interests; and, had he been even more rough and coarse, she perpetually avowed that she was not nice. 'She was,' said Walpole, 'main good at pumping; preferred to know everything, even though the knowledge shocked and pained her; was ready to enter into any scheme which seemed expedient, even though the furtherance of the scheme constrained her to abandon all self-respect.' But the chief agent between Walpole and the Queen was Lord Hervey, who filled an office in the household during that part of George the Second's reign in which Walpole was minister.

Hervey, then eldest son of the Earl of Bristol, was a man of considerable accomplishments, of great acuteness, and ready wit. Most people know of him by Pope's bitter lines, in which he is caricatured under the name of Sporus. They had been friends, and had quarrelled. Pope belonged, as far as his nature allowed him to entertain political feelings, to the Prince's party, as he had belonged to Atterbury's, to the alliance of which Shippen and Wyndham and Pulteney and Barnard were the heads. Hervey had a personal quarrel with the Prince, and was therefore willing enough to exasperate the enmity between the King and his heir; between the royal family and their prospective tyrant. His singularly weak constitution constrained him to live the life of an anchorite, in days when men habitually drank to excess. It made him popular with the ladies of the household, in whose company he was sober as well as agreeable. His beverage was tea, which Lord Bristol said poisoned him. At last, he became almost necessary to the Queen, who could hardly bear the loss of his amusing company for a day, and to the Princess Caroline, who was believed to entertain even tenderer feelings towards him. He played his part, that of alternate trifling and seriousness, with great skill, and was as useful to Walpole as he was agreeable to his mistress. As a narrator of Court gossip he is without a rival. His memoirs are a series of cabinet pictures, drawn, as he admits, in grotesque, and coloured more highly than the facts would seem to less interested parties.

How strange the scene appears to us! The Queen is dressing, attended by Lady Suffolk or Lady Sundon; the Princess Caroline putting in a word now and then; and the Princess Emily pouting by the fire. Hervey, pallid and painted, is relating gossip, or discussing some fresh affront of the Prince, or commenting on the tactics of the Patriots, or on the King's intrigues, and being bidden by the Queen not to call too much attention to his reputation as an *esprit fort*, but to speak low, because from the ante-chamber and through the half-closed door come the voices of the royal chaplains reading the daily service. One of these chaplains, less courtly than the rest, stopped when the door was too nearly closed; and on being asked why he did not go on, answered that he would not whistle the word of God through a keyhole. How inexpressibly soothing, to use the phrase of a distinguished divine of our day, must have been the service of the Establishment in those times; or rather what a hideous farce was the whole business, and how little need we wonder that such a social system developed monsters such as Stone and Blackburn, and later on, Cornwallis and Tomline, were.

It is generally understood that Walpole managed the House of Commons by bribery; that the secret service-money was thus employed: and that this minister was the father of that corruption which was reported to have disgraced the House during the first half of the last century. I suspect that these influences have been exaggerated. It is a stock story that Walpole said he knew every man's price. It might have been generally true, but the foundation of this apophthegm is, in all likelihood, a recorded saying of his about certain members of the Opposition. But Walpole knew well enough that he could not have bought Shippen, or Wyndham, or Pulteney, or any among the tribe of their followers. There were venal members then, as, in other forms, there are venal members now.

The fact is, there were a host of places in the civil list, which were given away for political support, and resumed for political apostacy, or even the suspicion of apostacy. Before the Place Bill of 1743, the House swarmed with pensioners. Every commission in the army or navy was conditional, and the holder of it might be turned adrift at the King's pleasure. The great Pitt, when a cornet in the Guards, was broken for ridiculing the King's negotiations about the Prince's marriage. Lord Pembroke paid £10,000 for a troop in the Guards, and was as summarily deprived of it without compensation. Social position, interest, and fear, kept the House docile; just as in our own days the expenditure of an election has been used as a threat against malcontents and remonstrants. In the later years of his administration, Walpole complained to Hervey that the King weakened his power by keeping army nominations exclusively in his own hands, and thereupon by making the army independent of the minister. 'How many people there are,' he said (in the crisis of

Pulteney's motion for increasing the Prince's allowance) 'whom I could bind to me by getting things done in the army, you may imagine.' But the King was obstinate on this point, though by doing as he did, he disobliged the very men whom it was highly important to conciliate, ultimately led the way to Walpole's fall, and helped to create the danger in which his crown was placed by the events of 1745.

In those days the clergy had great power, especially in the county elections. Since the fall of Atterbury, the Government had taken the utmost care to prevent any see from being filled by any disaffected person. But capacity might induce independence. Hence, with the exception of Butler, there is hardly a single prelate during this period of ecclesiastical history who was distinguished either for ability, learning, or piety; though there were many who scandalized even that age. But these prelates were employed, and as it seems successfully, by Walpole, in keeping the country clergy in good temper. To maintain this good temper, it was of course necessary that no concessions should be made to religious liberty, or even to justice. With such an understanding, Walpole opposed the repeal of the Occasional Conformity Act, and contrived to baffle all attempts to repeal the Test and Corporation Acts.

The Protestant Dissenters had been firm friends to the Hanoverian succession. The most intelligent among them declined the insidious Indulgence of James the Second, and after his abdication remained staunch to the principles of the Revolution. The laws enforced against them after the Restoration were abrogated or suffered to sleep when the era of responsible government began. Once, and once only, was there a reaction, when the Tories of Queen Anne's later years contrived in 1711 to pass the stringent Act to which I have several times alluded, an Act which was repealed after seven years' existence. In course of time, the Dissenters claimed the repeal of the Test and Corporation Acts. But again Walpole could not venture on gratifying them. He induced Hoadley to mediate between them and him. The conference between this prelate, who seems to have exacted his succession to the see of Winchester as the price of his good offices, was managed by King and Newcastle on the part of Government, and by a Committee of London Dissenters on behalf of the Nonconformists. Ultimately the Dissenters gave way. The time was not, or did not seem, ripe for this concession to justice and toleration. The force of the claim was weakened by its failure in 1730, and it took nearly a century to achieve it in the long run. Walpole's policy in dealing with the clergy was a very simple rule; 'whoever,' he said, 'would govern any body of men must appear to be in their interest.' The precedent has been followed in our own experience.

If the English prelates were good for little, the Irish were good for nothing. The impudent profligacy of Primate Stone, for which we must ransack the annals of the French Regency to find historical parallels, is even yet remembered in Ireland. But this creature had a sort of conscience. Lord Pembroke, it is reported, used to blaspheme so constantly and so violently at tennis, that Stone said it was as much as his character was worth to continue playing with him. Swift criticised the Irish appointments in his customary vein. 'The English Government,' he said, 'meant to appoint good bishops, but these people after nomination were invariably robbed by footpads on leaving London, and these fellows, not content with rifling their pockets and luggage, stole their clothes and patents as well, and posted to Ireland in their stead.'

During the last twenty years of the seventeenth century and the first forty of the eighteenth, England grew rapidly in material wealth. The value of land rose enormously. Great improvements were made in agriculture by the introduction of winter roots and artificial grasses. Farmers began to understand the rotation of crops. As a consequence, population increased largely. In 1700, the inhabitants of England and Wales were below five millions, in 1750, there is reason to believe that they had reached nearly double that number. This fact explains the rapid increase in the rentals of the aristocracy. Notwithstanding this growth, England exported large quantities of corn, wheat being so cheap during the first half of the eighteenth century, as to bring about the impression in the mind of so acute an observer as

Adam Smith, that silver had materially risen in value. But the fact is, the era was one of general prosperity. Added to this progress at home, was that of the plantations in the tropical and semi-tropical colonies. Mischievous as the process of cultivation was in them, and foolish as the colonial policy was, the product was so abundant as to far more than compensate for these social and economical errors. Besides, the wealth of foreign and colonial trade was added to the home prosperity of agriculture and manufacture. Of course the planter and the nabob were the most conspicuous among those wealthy upstarts, who were satirised at the time. The most obvious and natural use which they found for their money was in gorgeous equipages, in the purchase of parliamentary next presentations, or of political advowsons, and in the employment of these means for the end of obtaining hereditary place and rank in the great council of the nation.

It does not seem, however, that the prosperity of the country was distributed as effectually as it was produced. The rich were luxurious and extravagant, and they were emulated by their inferiors in wealth. There was no police whatever, and the country, the suburbs, even London, swarmed with footpads and highwaymen. There is no great amount of romance in the beggars' opera. Men were trained to the profession by adepts, who never let go the end of the rope which they gave their pupils. Fielding's grim history of Jonathan Wild the great is no gross exaggeration. But there was an aristocracy of birth and wealth. Aristocracies are always mercilessly cruel. The only schools they kept were the gaols, their only discipline was transportation and the halter. Death was inflicted for almost every offence. Under an aristocracy, whether it be of nobles or planters, property is the most sacred, human life the vilest thing, and in the Georgian Era, men and women were hanged in squads. The only terror which the legislature thought would be effectual under this sanguinary code, was that of shortening the time between sentence and execution. Writing to his friend from his modern Gothic villa of Strawberry Hill, Horace Walpole says: 'Seventeen were hanged this morning. One is forced to travel, even at noon, as if one were going to battle.' These laws in favour of property and caste had a very tenacious vitality. As a young child, I remember being taken to see the grave—how fresh I cannot recollect—of a man who had been hanged at Winchester for stealing fish out of a stew. This social discipline has passed away for a generation and a half. But it would be a folly to conclude that its effect has been effaced, or to imagine that the brutality of the law has not produced lasting results on the nature of the people.

Walpole has been designated, and with justice, as emphatically a peace minister. He held 'that the most pernicious circumstances in which this country can be, are those of war, as we must be great losers while the war lasts, and cannot be great gainers when it ends.' He kept George the Second at peace, as well as he could, by insisting on it that the safety of his dynasty lay in avoiding foreign embroilments. He strove in vain against the war which broke out in 1739, when the South Sea merchants, or, to be more correct, smugglers, in violation of the Assiento contract, goaded the nation into resisting the right of search which that treaty involved, and roused them to madness by the story of Jenkins' ears; Jenkins, the Don Pacifico of the eighteenth century. So passionately eager were the mercantile classes for war, that when it was proclaimed on October 19, 1739, the Stocks rose. When the bells were rung in joy at the war, Walpole cried, 'You ring the bells now, you will soon be wringing your hands.' He had work to do in checking those influential people, who, as Lord Grantham did, with earnest patriotism and bad grammar, continually shouted out, 'I hate the French, and I hope as we shall beat the French.'

That Walpole had a rational dislike for war, because he believed that it could always be avoided, and that its contingent advantages could never compensate for a tithe of the evils which it inevitably induces, is plain. He knew that a ministry which undertakes such a responsibility, however popular it is at first, is sooner or later unpopular; sooner, if the war policy be undertaken by error of judgment; later, even if the war policy be justified by the vulgar arts of demagogism. He was too sensible and honest a financier to carry on wars, as the elder Pitt almost exclusively did, by loans; and he knew therefore that it was no easy matter to find current funds. But he had a personal reason for his peace policy. He loved power, and he was strongly convinced that if he were forced or cajoled into war, he would inevitably be supplanted by one of those cheap heroes whom chance always thrusts to the front, and ignorance as regularly invests with every capacity and every virtue.

I do not intend to disparage Walpole's administrative ability, when I say that the country prospered independently of any financial policy which he adopted or carried out. This is a matter of easy illustration. In the last year of the seventeenth century Liverpool was a small town. A quarter of a century, and it was the third port in the kingdom, ranking after London and Bristol. In the same period the population of Manchester doubled; a similar growth took place in Birmingham. The Plantations in America and the Antilles flourished exceedingly. Walpole let matters take their course, for he understood that the highest merit of a minister consists in his doing no mischief.

But Walpole's praise lies in the fact, that, with this evident growth of material prosperity, he steadily set his face against gambling with it. He resolved, as far as lay in his power, to keep the peace of Europe; and he was seconded in his efforts by Cardinal Fleury. He contrived to smooth away the difficulties which arose in 1727; and on January 13,

1730, negotiated the treaty of Seville, the benefits of which lasted through ten years of peace, and under which he reduced the army to five thousand men. His domestic legislation was less successful. His excise scheme failed, owing, it is plain, to the factious opposition of the Patriots; his plan for creating bonded warehouses for storing goods (the duty being unpaid till such time as they were removed for consumption), also failed, owing to the interested opposition of the great mercantile houses, while he himself, apparently from administrative jealousy, resisted Sir John Barnard's scheme for reducing the interest on the public debt from four to three per cent.

Long before he resigned office, he was, or affected to be, weary of his work. 'I am plagued,' he said, 'with the thorns, and glutted with the fruits of power.' 'Few men,' he reiterated, 'should be ministers of state, for they see too much of the badness of mankind.' He really believed himself necessary to the security of the Protestant succession, to the peace of Europe, to the prosperity of the nation. He had, and events proved that he was right, the meanest opinion of those who must needs succeed him. He predicted their policy as accurately as he divined their motives and estimated their abilities; and he did all he could, during the three years in which he survived his official life, to thwart or sustain them, as occasion required. It was natural for a cynic like Lord Hervey, when Walpole stated his own opinion of his own value to the country, to comment, that 'acute and intelligent as this minister was, he was unable to discern that nobody's understanding is so much superior to the rest of mankind, as to be missed in a week after he is gone.'

Walpole had scanty knowledge of books or letters. He read very little, and wrote less. He carried into Parliament a little smattering of school learning, and was fond of quoting Horace. But though he quoted like a statesman, he knew his book only like a schoolboy. On one occasion he misstated a passage, committing a grammatical error for which in his youth he would have been birched. He was corrected by Pulteney, stuck to his version, wagered a guinea that he was right, and agreed to refer the dispute to the clerk of the House of Commons. Of course it was given against him, and he chucked the coin he had lost across the floor to his critic and antagonist. 'This,' said Pulteney, ' is the only guinea I ever got from the Government.'

According to those who knew him best, Walpole invariably kept to one rule on all public questions. 'He never would, be the wrong ever so extensive, and the circumstances ever so flagrant, allow, to the best of his power, parliamentary inquiries.' The rule has been adopted by later statesmen, who have applied it as much to cover their own misdeeds, as to save an existing administration in critical times. It has now become a tradition of cabinets. But resistance to it is the duty of those whose interests are involved in government, from the shareholders in a joint-stock company to the citizens of a community. The only guarantee of public honour is publicity, for the only protection rogues have is secresy.

Macaulay has commented on Walpole's contempt for letters, and has argued that the decline of literature during the period of Walpole's administration was due to this minister's indifference to literary men. But the discouragement is probably overstated. Pope was wealthy, thanks in the first instance to Swift's patronage. Gay, who had lost his money in the South Sea scheme, was protected by the mad Duchess of Queensberry. The Opposition was not unwilling to encourage the writers of their party. But literature, like other phenomena of productive energy, has its cycles of barrenness, its poor and abundant crops. The strife of faction however made the fortune of one genius. George the Second hated music and poetry. It is said that he professed to have admired one orchestral passage, and that its repetition was ordered. The players went through their pieces. At last they began to tune their fiddles, and George shouted out in ecstasy, that now they were playing what he liked. But to spite his son, he made Handel's fortune, though he expressed his contempt at this rivalry of fiddlers, this contest between tweedledum and tweedledee. 'The heat which this musical strife provoked, bade fair,' says Horace Walpole, 'to recall the green and blue factions of the Eastern Empire.' For a time, an anti-Handelist was looked on as an anti-courtier.

In 1741, a motion was made in both Houses, the object of which was to advise Walpole's dismissal from office. It was lost in the lower House by more than two to one; in the upper by nearly an equal majority. In the new Parliament, the veteran minister counted on a majority of forty. In a very short time, he was contemplating the alternatives of Downing Street and the Tower. The first discomfiture was the election of Dr. Lee as Chairman of Committees, in opposition to Earle, Sir Robert's candidate. He was beaten by four votes, and you can guess, says an eyewitness, how the victors huzza'd, after being defeated for twenty years. The old Duchess of Marlborough was denied the satisfaction of seeing this reverse. She was on her deathbed, and apparently insensible. 'She must be blistered,' said her physician, 'or she will die.' 'I won't be blistered,' she shouted out, with her last remains of strength, 'and I won't die.'

After Walpole's resignation came the struggle. He took an earldom, and secretly a pension. His eldest son had been made a peer in 1723. He got his natural daughter by Miss Skerrett—he married the mother—the rank and title of an earl's daughter. The victors resolved to punish him. Their first attempt failed by 253 votes to 250, the largest number, it is said, which was ever told in the old House. Sick—even dying members were brought into the vote. One of these members had lost an only son at sea, and the news had not reached him.

It was kept a secret till he was in the House, and then told him. But he did not flinch. Horatio Walpole, the minister's brother, had an official residence as Auditor of the Exchequer, from which a private door led into the House of Commons. He was on the point of bringing two or three sick members in, through this door, but found that the Opposition had shot the bolt, and filled the lock through the keyhole, with fine sand. The Prince still urged Walpole's impeachment, and a motion for a committee to inquire into the conduct of the last twenty years, was lost by 244 to 242, on March 9. On March 23, the attack was renewed, and a committee of twenty-one was carried—to be appointed by ballot—by 245 to 242. Then the struggle was to put Walpole's friends on the committee. They only succeeded in nominating five. But the Opposition was either satisfied or exhausted; the inquiry came to nothing, and Walpole was suffered to retire in peace. Of course the Duke of Newcastle, the patron of so many boroughs, gave additional proofs of his clumsy duplicity, and was the glad go-between to Pulteney.

Walpole died a poor man. His debts, including a few trifling legacies, amounted to £50,000. His estate was nominally worth £8000 a year, but was heavily mortgaged. In fact his fondness for Houghton had endangered its possession. He had not, like the Percevals and the Pelhams, built up a fortune out of public money. He was coarse and hard enough, but not sordid. Nor did he use more cruelty than policy—according to the judgment of the day—required. He urged the condemnation of the Scotch lords in 1716. But the Tower was so negligently guarded, that Nithsdale and Wintour escaped from it, perhaps with his connivance. Had he lived and kept office, the rising of 1745 would probably never have occurred. Had it occurred, he would have tempered the severities which followed it, which roused a dangerous sympathy for the sufferers, half justified the University of Oxford in paying for a picture of Flora Macdonald, and fastened on William, King George's favourite son, the nickname of the Cumberland butcher. It was to this William that Walpole gave his last piece of advice. The Duke consulted him as to how he should best be able to avoid a marriage with a Danish princess. 'Ask the King,' said Walpole, 'for an establishment, and he will not press it.' So the Duke escaped, married to please himself, gave occasion to the Royal Marriage Act, and is now chiefly remembered as the presumed progenitor of the Princess Olive, about whom our fathers gossiped, and of Mrs. Ryves, about whom our own generation has talked.

ADAM SMITH.

Bastiat; the experimental aspect is, and long will be, imperfect. The former has had little practical effect on the conduct of public affairs, exact and suggestive as the theory is, for it has constantly been disfigured by errors and paradoxes, and is distasteful from its very dogmatism; the latter has grown with the expansion of political experience, financial skill, social progress. The former may be condensed into a brief treatise; the latter is, as a coherent system, still buried in a vast accumulation of statistics, a mountain of unarranged and unexpounded facts. If you read the works of a French economist, the very best of the school, you will find abundant illustrations from fictitious hypotheses. If you open a page of Adam Smith, you will be sure to light upon a fact, an historical parallel, a careful induction.

I must say a few words on this ancient French economist, whose name has probably been heard by you for the first time this evening. As was the case with nearly every man of letters in that age, Oresme was an ecclesiastic. For some years he was Master of one of the Colleges in the University of Paris, and became successively Archdeacon of Bayeux, Dean of Rouen, Treasurer of Sainte Chapelle, and ultimately, in 1377, Bishop of Lisieux in Normandy. At some time or other he was Preceptor to Charles V, surnamed the Wise. The ordinary date given for his appointment to this office is impossible, for in 1360, Charles had no time for any other instruction than that in the school of adversity and patience. In

1356 occurred the battle of Poitiers, or Maupertuis, as it is now the fashion to call it, and during the interval between this catastrophe, and the Peace of Bretigni, Charles was the wandering regent of a shattered and debilitated kingdom, while his father was a prisoner in the Savoy. But 1360 may well have been the date of Oresme's treatise, 'On the Function of Money.'

There was ample necessity at that crisis for the promulgation of a sound theory on this subject. The privilege of coining money is conferred on an administration in order that the subjects of a government may be, as far as possible, protected from private fraud. The legend of the Maltese money ran—*non æs sed fides*—designating that the basis of the currency must be laid in the integrity of those who issue it. Yet hardly a European government fulfilled this duty, even if they understood and acknowledged it. But the Kings of France were the principal offenders. They diminished the amount of silver in their coins. This is a temporary wrong, a remediable offence. But they debased it also, a far more serious and lasting evil. Philip the Fair was threatened with excommunication by Boniface the Eighth, for this fraud, and was branded as long as time lasts, by Dante, for his offence. Even Thomas Aquinas, the Angelic Doctor, remonstrated with the French monarchs and denounced their practices. Seldom have excommunication and reproof been more richly merited, more justly launched.

But the greatest offender in this particular was the unlucky John, the prisoner of Poitiers, whose chivalric character has been described by Froissart, and lauded in a hundred romances. Nothing, in my opinion, points out more clearly the terrible gap which divided the knight from the peasant, during the fourteenth century, than the contrast between this monarch's historical reputation and his actual deserts. Owing to this King's practices, whom the romancers called the Good, the value of the currency underwent seventy changes in ten years. John took an oath of his moneyers that they would keep his frauds a profound secret, especially from the merchants, and would do their diligence to deceive the public, with a threat that, if they gave an opportunity of detection, they should suffer the penalties of treason. There have been times when sentimental novelists have striven to harmonise the lighter and darker shades of character in heroes like Claud Duval, Paul Clifford, Eugene Aram, and Jack Sheppard. It is to such panegyrists that we may relegate the task of describing a monarch, who might have been a gallant knight on the battle-field, but who was a smasher in his own mint, a swindler of his people. It was these practices which Oresme reprobated.

I have already commented on the fact, that historians are apt to overlook the economical side of their subject. This folly or negligence, as it comes from the mannerism which Macaulay used to ridicule as concessions to the 'dignity of history,' or from sheer ignorance, leaves us constantly in the dark as to the real causes which aid the progress or hurry the downfall of nations. To me the weakness of France during the century 1340–1440, seems to be directly traceable to economical causes, to the universal distrust which these royal frauds induced. All nations, as they emerge from barbarism, adopt a currency, the circulation of which is conditioned by a few intelligible principles. A man takes money to get rid of it, because it facilitates exchange, and is of all commodities that which is most easily sold. But to facilitate exchange and to be easily sold, it must be, for a time at least, possessed of an intrinsic, unchangeable value, and must be capable of instant valuation. To debase the currency is to destroy the very essence of its utility, and to force society back into barbarism and isolation. Exactly similar results, though perhaps of a less serious kind, attended, as I stated in a previous lecture, the frauds of Henry the Eighth and the Protector Somerset. Results of an analogous kind always follow, in various degrees, those unhappy concessions to the nostrums of such currency quacks, as persuade governments to commit an offence to which they are only too prone, the issue of paper money on the security of public debts.

It was because there is no part of the theory of political economy which is so strictly logical as the demonstration of the function which money performs in civilised society, and because the same or nearly the same exactness belongs to the exposition of the process by which wealth is produced, that the French economists have been so successful in these two parts of the science. It is when they come to deal with the phenomena of exchange, with the influence which custom or conventional usage has upon social life, and with the circumstances which modify the distribution of wealth, that their system breaks down for want of induction, and because they adopt hypotheses instead of facts. They construct a formal garden, the plants of which they select, and the cultivation of which they arrange, and neglect to study the pasture which lies outside this factitious parterre, and in which nature supersedes art. For the study of political economy—the latest and the most difficult of the sciences—is the estimate of society and politics from the vast aggregate of experience, as it denotes the causes which direct or control the industrial energies of different communities, and attempts to discover the circumstances under which the material interests of social life vary in kind or in degree.

What little we know of the personal history of Adam Smith is from the pen of Dugald Stewart, and was composed a few years after this great economist had ended his quiet uneventful life. The posthumous son of a Custom-house officer at Kirkcaldy, he was carefully brought up by his mother, whose years were extended to within six of his own death, and who constantly lived with her illustrious son, as she was affectionately tended by him. Smith received his first teaching in his native town, at one of those schools which were even then of infinite value to Scotchmen, and the establishment of which was of primary interest and care to the founders of the Scotch Reformation. When he was fourteen years old, he was transferred to the University of Glasgow.

During the reign of Charles the Second, a Glasgow merchant, zealous to maintain Episcopacy in Scotland, granted funds towards the establishment of exhibitions in Balliol College, Oxford, the recipients of this benefaction being chosen out of the students of the Glasgow University, and by that Corporation. A few years afterwards, Episcopacy fell, but the benefaction remained, and grew considerably in value. There are ten such exhibitions held by students of Balliol College, and there is no doubt that the great reputation of this Academical society is due in no slight degree to the annual selection of some of the most promising young Scotchmen at Glasgow for further instruction in a College which is peculiarly connected with Scotland. When he was seventeen years old Adam Smith was nominated to one of these exhibitions, and proceeded to Oxford, where he resided, it seems, uninterruptedly for seven years. But he never graduated at this University.

When Smith left Scotland for Oxford, his native country was miserably poor. The annalists of British commerce, Anderson and Macpherson, have very little to tell us of Scotland's trade and manufactures.

A linen manufacture existed in the Lowlands, and especially on the eastern coast, but it was of small proportions. For the greater part of the eighteenth century Scotland sent no revenue to the Imperial treasury, the scanty proceeds of taxation being swallowed up in local charges and bounties. It took five or six days to travel from Aberdeen to Edinburgh. The country gentlemen resented the Methuen treaty, and the scarcity of claret, and entered into arrangements with smugglers for a supply of French wines and brandies. In 1745, Duncan Forbes, Lord President of Session, wrote to the Elgin justices and urged them 'not to be so impudently profligate as to screen these offenders,' wishes to know 'how they individually vote in favour of, or against, repressing this evil, in order that he may know what scoundrels to detest and avoid,' and concludes a long letter of reproach and warning by 'making his compliments to every one among them, who can lay his hand on his heart, and say that he is not a rascal.' Ten years after this a letter printed by Captain Dunbar informs us that there is no news, as the Edinburgh mail-bag was returned in a mistake for the London mail and vice versa.

The lairds in the Highland districts exercised heritable jurisdiction. A gallows was a regular part of the buildings on the estate, a hangman always figured in the chieftain's retinue, unless, like Sir Robert Gordon, the laird found it more convenient to drown his local culprits. Death was inflicted for

petty thefts, imprisonment awarded without warrant
or prospect of release, except when the local magnate
was pacified. The peasantry seem to have acquiesced,
or at most to have avenged themselves only by
making strange charges of sorcery against their lords.
These rights were abolished after the affair of 1745,
not, it seems, because they were deemed unreasonable
in themselves, but because they were abused, and
made subservient to rebellion. Slavery, however, prevailed in Scotland till after Smith's death, for the
Colliers and Salters, who were excepted by name
from the Scotch Habeas Corpus Act of 1701, were
only finally emancipated in 1799.

If the rural districts were thus under the dominion
of the lairds, who had appropriated the land of their
clansmen, and had engrafted a rigid system of entails
on the ancient tenures of the country, the boroughs
were in no better plight. The property and revenues
of these boroughs, the right of local taxation, patronage, jurisdiction, and the election of representatives
to Parliament, were in the hands of small self-elected
bodies. Droll stories are told of the way in which
this patronage was sold or distributed. For example,
the office of town-clerk at Forfar was held for twenty
years by an idiot. In 1831, the county voters in the
whole of Scotland were only 2500, many of whom
had neither property nor residence in the county for
which they held the franchise. The electors in the
sixty-six boroughs amounted to 1440 only. Thirty-
three electors returned the representatives for Glas-

gow and Edinburgh. We can under these circumstances understand the Scotch member who boasted that he had never been present at a debate or absent at a division, and that he had only once voted conscientiously, and then found that he was in the wrong. Nor again can we wonder that even as late as 1820, when there was a sharp contest between the families of Grant and Duff for the representation of the Elgin burghs, the Duffs kidnapped the baillie of Elgin, and a Mr. Dick, two of the opposite side, and carrying them off to Sutherlandshire, kept them there till it was too late to vote. The character of these Scotch municipalities was retained unchanged till 1833. But we need not be surprised that when the change was made, a Marquis of Bute moved that the Scotch Municipalities Reform Bill should be read that day six months, and that an Earl of Haddington entered his protest on the journals of the Lords, and predicted all sorts of danger to the constitution from the change.

Towards the close of Adam Smith's life Dundas ruled despotically in Scotland. Three years after his death, Muir was prosecuted for sedition, the words which he used being what is now every-day criticism on existing administrations. Braxfield, the Jeffreys among Scotch judges, raged in the style of Jeffreys, a hundred years after such a monster became impossible on the English bench. 'Bring me prisoners,' he shouted, 'and I will find them law.' And when a pliant jury convicted Muir, he inflicted an illegal sentence, adding that he increased the penalty because the audience applauded Muir's eloquent defence. The Liberals who, like Horner and Jeffreys and Brougham and Sidney Smith, dared to keep alive the principles of freedom in Edinburgh seventy years ago, imperilled their fortunes, their liberty, and even their lives, by their courage. What wonder that enfranchised Scotland has raised her monument on Calton Hill to the martyrs of the eighteenth century, and has all but entirely repudiated the principles which were dominant and despotic little more than a generation ago. In talking of the Reign of Terror in France, people forget that there was as frightful a reign of terror in Ireland, and that there were reactionary if not revolutionary tribunals in Great Britain during the same epoch.

Mr. Macculloch, without stating his reasons, avers that Smith does not appear to have felt any peculiar respect for the great University at which he completed his education. I am not aware that he speaks of his personal relations to it except in one passage, where, acknowledging his election as Lord Rector of Glasgow, he mentions it as part of his debt of gratitude to that institution, that it sent him to Oxford. In truth, it cannot be doubted that however other people may have conducted themselves at Oxford, Smith derived great advantage from his studies there. His reputation in his native country was acknowledged immediately on his return. The fact is, just as eminent scholars have, from time to time, proceeded from Eton, because diligence and genius will exhibit themselves under the most untoward circumstances, so men could study with profit even in that, the darkest age of Academical history. There is reason for calling that a dark age. There is a consistent tradition of the period during which Smith lived in Oxford, to the effect that an enterprising cat was found in All Souls' library, but starved to death, and dried into a mummy. All Souls' had the best college library in Oxford, owing to the nugatory munificence of Codrington.

With one notable exception, that of the wonderful Puritan movement of the sixteenth and seventeenth centuries, which sprang from Mildmay's College in Cambridge, every great upheaval in learning, politics, and religion, which England has witnessed, has had its beginnings in Oxford. It was there that Merton, during the calm revolution of Henry the Third's reign, began to establish a system of secular learning, by excluding all monks and friars from the benefit of his, the earliest English college. The fruit of this policy is to be seen in the fact, that, within a century after this foundation, Wiklif, the bitter enemy of the monastic orders and the great ecclesiastics, learned his power of controversy within the walls of Merton's College. To counteract Wiklif's doctrine, another College was founded, from which, three centuries afterwards, came even a greater reformer than Wiklif. At the close of the fifteenth century, Oxford was the birthplace of physical science, and the early nurse of that revived classical learning which supplied the longings after ecclesiastical reformation with critical powers, for Linacre, the first English physiologist, Colet, Erasmus, More, the earliest students of classical scholarship, were among her sons. In those days, the energies of the University were not straitened by an Act of Uniformity.

After the great shock of the Reformation in Europe, and the vast, well-nigh destructive changes which subsequently ensued, when both parties appealed to the sword, when liberty was sacrificed to municipal selfishness, and the quarrels of potentates begot that monstrous phantom, the balance of power, Oxford fell under the baneful influence of Laud. She did not indeed submit without a struggle. The Puritan party, dominant in Cambridge, was strong in Oxford. Nor was the High Church reaction a mere step into darkness. Laud, despite his blind bigotry, his slavish superstitions, his ungovernable temper, was a sincere lover of learning. He pensioned Chillingworth, and promoted Hales. But in great Academies, no patronage can compensate for the loss of freedom. Oxford was weakened by the discipline of Laud, and was demoralized by becoming the head-quarters of the Cavaliers. The Laudian regimen became the tradition of the University. Its Convocation, after the Restoration, solemnly proclaimed the divine right of Kings, and as solemnly proscribed the principles of human freedom. It clung to these tenets after the Revolution, and became the focus of the Jacobite faction. In the first half of the eighteenth century, it was the hiding-place of the Pretender's adherents. The Tory squires sent their sons to Oxford. The heads of Colleges and the heads of the University, made one by Laud's pernicious legislation, protected these boys, when they made the streets ring with curses on King George and blessings on King James. Sometimes soldiers were sent to keep these young rebels, and old traitors in awe. Then there was outward quiet, and the Academical authorities shut themselves up in their official lodgings, to write diaries, to complain of Hanoverian tyranny, to drink their port, and to symbolise their attachment to the fallen dynasty by passing their wine over the water-jug, while they swore allegiance to the ruling powers, on pain of losing their emoluments. In the very year in which Smith left Oxford, a treasonable riot occurred in the streets, the culprits being members of Balliol College. They were screened by Purnell, the Warden of New College and Vice-Chancellor. But Walpole cared little for these things. That minister, who is said to have held one tenet strongly, that every man has his price, was alive to another more general and more generous rule, that every fool should have his way. The audacity of these academics culminated, when, in 1734, the University complimented George the Second on the marriage of his daughter to the Prince of Orange, and hinted, as well as it could, on the blessings which a former Prince of Orange had been enabled to confer on the nation.

It will surprise no one to hear that this noisy disaffection was coupled with gross ignorance, and still more gross brutality. What the condition of education was in the old Universities during the eighteenth century, is plain from the novels of the period. The Professorships at Oxford were turned into sinecures. The occupants of those offices did not pretend to teach anybody. Even long after the period to which I refer, up to the time when Academical reform was seriously taken in hand fourteen years ago, hardly a fraction of the University professors undertook any active duty. Adam Smith's criticism on their utter uselessness in his time is well known.

The age was eminently coarse. But the fugitive literature of Oxford was more coarse than that which was current with the general public. Grub Street and Hog Lane would not have put forth such abominations as the speeches of *Terræ filius* or the rhymes on the Oxford Toasts. Nor was this brutality confined to words. I have spoken of the turbulence of those young men. In the very year in which Adam Smith left Oxford, the undergraduates of Balliol College murdered a college servant, under circumstances of the grossest barbarity. The narrative of this crime is to be found in a pamphlet written at the time, which, for grave and earnest comment on the atrocity, might have been written by Smith himself. The culprits were protected by Theophilus Leigh, Master of the College, who owed his election to an intrigue, and held his place for fifty-two years.

I said above that out of a college, founded for the express purpose of doing battle with the tenets propagated by the great reformer of the fourteenth century, came, exactly three centuries after the date of its foundation, a greater reformer. Perhaps at no age of the history of Christianity had all its vital principles fallen more completely into sleep than during the first half of the eighteenth century. Then began the revival inaugurated by the two Wesleys. The elder son of the rector of Epworth was a fellow of Lincoln College, and here established that enthusiastic movement which spread over the British Islands and many of her colonies. Wesley's influence, like all religious influences, was social also, and civilisation owes to him and his sectaries that they were, if not precisely the first, the most energetic and powerful preachers in that anti-slavery crusade, which gained its first legal victory in 1771, when the judges decided, in the case of Charles Somerset, that slavery cannot exist on British soil, and has nearly consummated its beneficent aims, after a century of uninterrupted struggles.

I will not dwell on the latest of these Academical developments; on what has been called the Tractarian movement, and last of all on the philosophical liberalism of Oxford in our own day. It is sufficient to point out how continuous has been the influence of Academical activity on English thought, and how far removed one English University is, at least, from the mere function of a schoolmaster in dead languages, and an extinct philosophy.

Originally Smith was destined for Anglican orders, the preparation of candidates for this office having been the original purpose of Snell's foundation. But he abandoned this prospect, returned to Scotland, lived a few years at Edinburgh, and in 1751 was appointed to a professorship at Glasgow. Here he remained for twelve years, when he accepted the post of travelling tutor to the young Duke of Buccleugh. Stewart laments that Smith arrived at that decision, and suggests that the interruption of his studies was a public loss. It would be more correct to say, that we owe the 'Enquiry into the Nature and Causes of the Wealth of Nations' to this interruption in his previous habits. The three years during which he travelled in France suggested to him the conception, and to some extent supplied him with the materials of his great work.

Adam. Smith visited France immediately on the conclusion of the Seven Years War. The Peace of Paris, which Sismondi says was the most humiliating which France had ever undergone since that of Bretigni, stripped her of her colonies in the New World, and her settlements and factories in the East. Lally had succumbed to Clive, Montcalm to Wolfe. England, on the other hand, was generally victorious.

But the victory was obtained by profuse expenditure. The public debt—for it was chiefly by loans that the war was sustained—was doubled under the elder Pitt's administration. One war begat another. The charges of the Seven Years War, when the reaction of peace came, were grievously oppressive, and the Government was at its wit's end for money. In an evil hour they resolved to tax the colonies by a stamp-duty, and to reimburse the East India Company for an advance to the treasury, by a duty on tea, to be levied on New England. Everybody knows the story of the resistance to the Stamp Act, of the riot in Boston harbour, of the Declaration and the War of Independence. The reaction of that war precipitated the French Revolution. The proclamation of the Duke of Brunswick gave that revolution the unity which it needed, and half justified its atrocities. It was followed by the great convulsion through which Europe passed at the beginning of the present century. The effects of this convulsion will not pass away for generations.

Two years after Smith quitted Paris, Corsica was ceded to France by the Genoese. The relations of Corsica and Genoa are a long story. They are in little, the parallel to the relations between the East India Company, India, and the British Empire. In her difficulties, the republic of Genoa had consulted her leading merchants on the state of her finances. The merchants—for, as a rule, mercantile credit is higher than the credit of a government—came to the rescue. They retrieved the finances, and received privileges for the Bank of Genoa in exchange. The Bank began to make war and acquire territory on its own account, after the fashion and the folly of the time, and conquered Corsica. It was the box of Pandora, without Hope at the bottom. Finding the possession mischievous, the Bank presented this pernicious estate to the Genoese republic. At the beginning of the eighteenth century, Genoa was in a state of chronic war with the savage islanders of Corsica, just as Turkey now is, with those of Crete. My hearers may remember the story of Theodore Neuhoff, who, in 1736, appeared at Aleria, as a mysterious stranger, whose riches seemed boundless to those barbarous people, how he was made king, and how, after checkered fortunes, he quitted the island, came to England, got up a new expedition, failed, returned to London, and was thrown into prison for debt, lived in prison there seven years, and when released by the despair of his creditors, was kept from starving by the efforts of Horace Walpole, and how at last he died in such poverty, that Walpole could contrast the fallen monarch's experience of the possession of a kingdom and the want of bread in a couplet. Too late, Paoli came to the rescue. After the Peace of Paris, the Genoese sold the island to France, despite the intrigues of North. It was the worst bargain which the house of Bourbon ever made, for a twelvemonth after the sale was completed, Napoleon was born, a French subject, and the founder of a dynasty which has certainly dethroned the Bourbons, and may hereafter extinguish royalty in France. The story of Œdipus is rivalled, by the efforts which Louis XV made to annex Corsica to France.

Certainly, if the maxims of good government can be best learned by witnessing the consequences of their violation, no better study could be found for the economist than the condition of France at this time. Four assemblies, called parliaments, sat in four places. There was no true commercial intercourse between the several provinces of the kingdom. The lands of the nobles and the church were free from taxation; those of the peasants were afflicted by an arbitrary *taille* and an equally arbitrary *corvée*. Agricultural improvement was impossible when an income-tax was levied on the visible means of the farmer—just as it is in Ireland, wherever the rent is raised to the highest possible amount by letting annual tenancies by auction. All grades in the army were closed to those who were not ennobled; all industry was harassed by arbitrary restrictions. The King's officers were petty but absolute tyrants, and tyranny is always most grinding when it is exercised in a narrow area and on few victims. The criminal law, as is always the case under despotic governments, be they monarchical or aristocratic, was frightfully severe. Sudden and secret arrest was everybody's risk; torture was freely adopted in order to obtain convictions; and punishment was inflicted with every refinement which a diabolical ingenuity could inflict. Our government, during the same epoch, was savage enough, was unrelenting, Draconian in its attempts to protect property by the free use of the gallows; but the French of the eighteenth century are said to have united the manners of monkeys to the ferocity of tigers. The execution of Damiens, for example, was prolonged through hours of torture.

Political servitude is the parent of atheism; for men cease to believe in God when all they know of government is despotism, when they cannot recognise God's moral qualities in man, and when religion is parodied by its professed teachers. Again, it cannot be by accident that sceptics in religion are absolutists in politics. This combination has been witnessed over and over again. Spinoza and Hobbes, Bolingbroke and Hume, are only a few instances out of many. In the middle of the eighteenth century the Encyclopædists represented this form of fatalism. 'The French,' said a gentleman to an eminent scholar and wit, 'worship Voltaire as some men worship Christ.' 'And a very good Christ for a Frenchman,' was the reply. Join an acutely logical mind to an irreverent wit, fluent sentiment to a selfish heart, elegant taste to utter depravity, and smother the whole with unsleeping and exuberant vanity, and you get the French gentleman of the old monarchy. Voltaire was a little better, and Rousseau a little worse, than this model. Such people were fairly imitated in England by

Chesterfield and Horace Walpole. The example was repeated in its coarser and more revolting traits by Wilkes and Sandwich, and the rabble of the Medmenham monks.

The head of the French social system, of a troop of profligate courtiers, and still more profligate churchmen, was Louis XV. Brought up in the midst of flatterers, accustomed to indulge every caprice, he was utterly unable to reason; habituated to indulge in every excess, his life was one long orgie. 'His religious belief,' says Sismondi, 'consisted in his dread of the Divine vengeance, and in the dogma of his own absolute power.' As he grew older, he grew worse. From Versailles to the Parc aux cerfs was one degradation, even for him; from Pompadour to Du Barry was another. But withal he was strictly orthodox. The victims of his vile pleasures were carefully instructed in the Catholic faith. Though he wallowed in every pollution, he was anxious to keep his harem free from the heresies of the Jansenists. His title was that of 'the most Christian king;' and, according to his interpretation of Christianity, he resolved to maintain his reputation. But in these days, no one could venture on telling, ever so superficially, the recorded details of his private life.

There was, however, in Paris a society with which Adam Smith became intimately acquainted. This was the sect of the Economists, and, in particular, Turgot, Quesnay, Dupont de Nemours. These men were theorists; but the motive-cause of their speculations was a very practical evil. They saw that agriculture was depressed, and that labour was degraded. It was no use to attack the fiscal system under which France groaned. The Government had a short and sharp remedy against those who offended it; and any attack, however indirect, on the privileges possessed by the nobles and the clergy, was a crime—the crime, namely, of exciting hatred and contempt against the Government. Now it could not be denied that the measure of population is determined by the success of agriculture, that the more subsistence the earth can be made to produce, the more persons can subsist, and, indirectly, the larger the amount of that which, under the name of rent, the owner of the soil can appropriate to himself. Conversely, the more the farmer pays to the state, the less can he pay to the landlord. But as all produce on which a price can be put is derived from the soil, and as all purchase is of such produce, to curtail a man's power of purchase is to check production, and to debar him from offering a price for such produce. But as rent is all that remains over and above the cost of producing that which the producer sells, it follows that to tax the purchaser is to diminish rent; and, therefore, as all taxes ultimately fall upon rent, the policy of the French fiscal system seemed to lay taxation on the farmer, but in reality to lay it on the landlord.

I will not occupy you with a dissertation on the

mixture of truth and error which this view of the economists contains. It is sufficient to point out that in distributing the gross price of any product other than those which are purely agricultural, the portion which is appropriated as rent is almost infinitesimal. But there is a more obvious answer still. The logical inference of this argument would be to tax the rent of land in order to supply the public revenue and local levies. But in this country, the annual amount of local and imperial taxation is considerably in excess of the whole rent of land.

The economists had another and a more rational purpose before them. Colbert, minister of finance in the early days of Louis XIV, saw the wealth which commerce and manufactures had bestowed on the Dutch, and sought to appropriate some portion of this prosperity to France. To effect this, he gave state assistance to manufacture, and, as far as France was concerned, was the founder of the mercantile system in that country. Like most theories, this had a true side in it. Manufacturing countries are generally wealthy, and for two reasons. The very existence of such industry proves that agriculture produces in excess over the needs of those who labour at it. Next, manufactures represent larger values in portable shape than agricultural products do, and can therefore be more easily transported and sold. The power which this country possessed during the great continental war consisted in the value of, and demand for, its manufactures, and the command which it thereupon had over the markets of the world. But the error of the French policy lay in the fact, that these advantages are easily seen, and when seen are certainly acted on; that the instinct of self-interest needs no stimulus, and that industry finds out its own good best. We have learned, but only lately, that a Government is the worst judge of the way in which the capital of those for whom it consults can be administered or invested. When Governments affect to help, they retard the progress they patronise.

Even here, however, the French theorists fell into a strange delusion. They argued that nature does nothing for man in manufactures, forgetting that the labour of man is busied in appropriating certain forms of matter and their qualities, by means of certain natural forces. To discuss whether nature does most for man in agriculture or manufactures, apart from the illogical distinction of processes not radically distinguishable, is to debate which of two scissor-blades contributes most to severing a piece of cloth. Adam Smith was not free from the fallacy into which his teachers fell, and the modern student is constantly able to detect the influence of the French theory on his mind, though on many occasions he refutes its errors.

That which Adam Smith got from the French economists was the habit of analytical research, exercised upon economical phenomena. I do not say that political economy began with him, but I can assert that its method does. His teachers argued from *à priori,* or what they believed to be *à priori,* principles, and examined the facts by these principles. Smith applied an inductive method to his facts, and, as far as possible, verified his hypotheses by observation. Hence his work is full of illustrations, is copious in examples, whenever illustration or example could be obtained. And just as succeeding economists have used his method, and in so far as they have gone to history and statistics, so they have been able to correct Smith; for in his day history was uncritical, statistics were imperfect and inexact. But in so far as they have departed from his method, and suffered themselves to evolve the science from their own theories, they have, even the ablest among them, fallen into notorious fallacies.

The quickness of Smith's inductive power was as noteworthy as his diligence in collecting materials where materials were forthcoming. For example, he was well aware that the mass of the English peasantry passed from a state of penury and dependence in the thirteenth century into one of affluence and prosperity in the fifteenth. The peasant in the first epoch, as described by the early English law-books, is a totally different person from the yeoman of Fortescue's age. Smith rightly divined that the mass of the agriculturists must have passed through a *métayer* system before they arrived at independence. And the facts recently discovered bear out this hypothesis. After the great social convulsion of the fourteenth century, the greatest which modern history has undergone,—due to the occurrence of the great plague in the year 1349,—it became impossible for the landowners to carry on their estates by hired labour, for the wages of labour rose at once by 50 to 100 per cent., and there had long existed a custom of commuting serf-labour, never very profitable, for a money payment. The attempt to revive this serf-labour led, beyond the shadow of a doubt, to the uprising of 1381, known familiarly as Wat Tyler's rebellion. In the interval, and indeed after this event, (for the demands of the Blackheath rioters were effectually conceded,) it became necessary for the landowners to let their lands. As the new tenants had not enough capital to stock these farms, (for in these days the stock on a well-tilled farm was worth three times as much as the land,) the landlord leased farm and stock together, on consideration of receiving a certain portion of the produce. This is the *métayer* system which has prevailed in Southern France, and generally in Italy from the days of Imperial Rome. In about seventy years, so great was the prosperity of the English yeomanry in those days, the farmer was able to carry on his business with his own stock, and, in many cases, to purchase the land on which he lived. I have supplied you with the verification of Smith's hypothesis, but the hypothesis itself is an induction of singular sagacity.

The hardest work which any writer or thinker has before him is to separate himself from the habitual and tyrannous prejudices of the age in which he lives.

A prejudice is a judgment, but an imperfect judgment. It is because it simulates an exact inference that the person who holds it, or, to be more correct, is occupied by it, is irritated at any attempt to disturb it. It is because attempts to disturb prejudice are generally made by the emission of other prejudices, the weak points of which are recognised by the adversary, that the attempt is constantly a failure. Even when the refutation of an error is overwhelming, men are not apt to be thankful to their instructor.

The dreamer in Horace, before whose eyes, as he sat in an empty theatre, and applauded what he thought were the scenes, the processions, the poetry of noble tragedies, had little thanks for his friends when they cured him of his delusion, and thereby took away the pleasure of his existence. 'During my whole life,' said a friend of Tooke the economist, 'I have been laboriously engaged in gathering and binding up my faggot of notions,—how can you expect that I shall be grateful to you for unloosing and scattering them away?' The fate of reformers is well known,—the indifference of lukewarm friends, the undisguised hostility of bitter enemies. As long as loss and injury are the portion of those who labour to speak wisely and do justly, there is no immediate risk of rash and sudden change. 'So you intend,' said a Yorkshire nobleman to Wilberforce, 'to reform society. I will show you the destiny of all reformers;' and he pointed to a picture of the Crucifixion.

It must be admitted that in Adam Smith's days,

when books were dear, and confined to the educated few, when there was no popular press, and no means for reaching and teaching the mass of the people, the intolerance of prejudiced authority was far less marked than it is in later times. Smith's political economy was a war against privilege and monopoly, as all honest political economy is, whether it be privilege on the part of landlords or masters, peasants or workmen. But it awakened no violent opposition, because it awakened no immediate fear. Smith was a Scotch professor, and the monopolists of the age felt no serious alarm at the speculations of a north country thinker. It is only in these later days that vested interests begin to dread and detest the intellectual activity of the 'wild men of the cloister.' I have indeed seen one violent attack on the 'Wealth of Nations' in the preface and notes of Mickle's Lusiad. But Mickle wished to get patrons for his work among the holders of East India Stock, and Smith had severely commented on the monopoly of the great Company. In Smith's time the manufacturers and merchants were the great advocates of protection, and Smith thought that they would cling to it with more tenacity than the agriculturists did to their bounties and corn laws. He was wrong. Thirty years after the great economist's death, Tooke drew up the memorable Merchants' petition. Simultaneously, and as if by contrast, Vansittart produced his last budget. It took more than a quarter of a century before the Corn Laws were abandoned, and they were given up under the pressure of a formidable agitation, and a frightful famine. The event was followed by the wreck of traditional parties, and the establishment of new parties under old names. Even now the battle of protection and freedom is being waged, though on a different material, and under a disguise, in the pressure of a similar crisis, and with the prospect of the same political phenomena.

In the days of Adam Smith statesmen thought that money was wealth, and that a country which permitted the export of the precious metals, unless indeed it produced them from its own mines, and in excess of its own wants, was wilfully inviting poverty. He demonstrated that money was distributed over the world just as all other merchandise is, and by the same machinery. We now know that all the perfection of the mechanism by which money fulfils the functions of currency, consists in the multitude of transactions which the least possible quantity of money can effect, and that communities strive as far as possible to economise the currency which they retain.

The statesmen of the age believed that it was a matter of paramount necessity that a country's exports should exceed its imports. Adam Smith developed the exactly opposite doctrine. He taught that a profitable trade consists in getting as much foreign goods as possible, with as little British goods as possible; that the difference between the two is the profit on the transaction; that the goods of one country are exchanged against the goods of another; and that the wisdom of the merchant is contained in finding the market in which he can sell at the highest price, and buy at the lowest. He therefore repudiated those expedients for securing a special market for British produce, which was in his day the main object of commercial diplomacy, and was till the time of Canning, who gave his instructions to our representative at the Hague, at that time negotiating certain concessions, in characteristic doggrel—

'In matters of commerce, the fault of the Dutch
Is giving too little, and asking too much.'

We now know that communities which hamper their foreign trade with restrictions deliberately choose the worst market for their produce.

The Economists taught that land was wealth. Adam Smith proved—and it was a prodigious step in advance—that labour was the cause and the sole cause of wealth. Everybody knows how he illustrated this position, and conclusively proved it, in his famous chapter on the division of labour. The importance of this distinction cannot be overrated, for it gave a scientific explanation of the origin of rent, and a scientific refutation of those communistic theories which anticipate the reform of all social inequalities and grievances by a redistribution of land. For as long as people believe, or perhaps are led to believe, that land is wealth, so long will they, seeing that its original distribution is accidental or arbitrary, claim as a matter of abstract justice, which needs only sufficient power to become a matter of legislative action, that such inequalities as have arisen from past circumstances should be rectified. The French economists of later times have never escaped from the influence of the thinkers who were associated with the early studies of Adam Smith, and therefore either argue, as Proudhon and others, that 'property is theft,' or with Bastiat and the school which he has founded, an equally untenable paradox, that 'all the value which land has acquired is the result of labour.'

Agrarian forms of socialism, disputes about what really constitutes property in land, and what the extent of that property is, have been the earliest causes of party strife in the social history of mankind. When communities subsist on agricultural produce, the necessity for defining this property becomes only more immediate and urgent than it does when the life of a people is spent in hunting and in pastoral pursuits. The battles of savage tribes are agrarian contests, in which the prize is the fairest hunting-ground. The progress of civilised life necessitates the abandonment of these savage forms of sustentation or amusement; though, so strangely are the extremes of habit continued, that, in a country like our own, it is still argued that the unlimited preservation of game is a legitimate and defensible practice, though it is clear that when any region which can be made to produce food by agricultural labour is abandoned to the maintenance of wild animals, it cannot supply a hundredth part of the food which it might otherwise afford.

They who have studied the early history of civilisation, are aware how incessant has been the ventilation of the agrarian question. It appears in the fierce municipal struggles of ancient Greece. It is the most distinct fact in the mythical annals of Rome. The customs of feudal Europe referred with hardly an exception to the determination of the rights which the possessor of property in land might exercise. The social question in Ireland, where, till within 250 years, the custom of Celtic tenures existed and was recognised, has been uninterruptedly agrarian. In our own country, where the limits of private ownership in land have perhaps been extended farther than in any other community, where private rights are conceded to the possessor more fully than elsewhere, the debate as to what must be the maximum of private ownership has been greatly aided by the interpretation of the circumstances which originally necessitate the ownership in question.

The joint or common ownership of land, enjoyed by the whole of any given society, is abandoned for particular or private ownership on economical grounds. When land is cultivated by spade or plough, it sustains many more people than could subsist on an equal area occupied by domesticated animals. But the cultivation of the soil is impossible except on the condition of permanent ownership. The man who ploughs and sows expects to reap, and will not plough and sow, unless the prospect of reaping is sufficiently guaranteed to him. In course of time, this guarantee becomes permanent. For other reasons, this permanent occupation represents annually a higher value than is sufficient to compensate for the charges of cultivation, and rent arises. Lastly, discretionary powers over land are accorded. But society cannot ever, except by an act of suicide, abandon the right of asking and answering the following questions. Does the occupation, the use, the distribution of land, subserve that purpose for which society originally abandoned its common right in the soil? Does the concession of these private rights, intended to effect the fullest productiveness of land, in any way militate against the end which it is always supposed to accomplish? These rights were granted in order to ensure the fertility of the soil; does the existing usufruct induce barrenness? Is it always clear that private interest is sufficiently strong to prevent the waste of these powers, which are, after all, part of the national resources? Upon these and similar questions, the economical interpretation of the theory of rent and the distribution of land has given and is giving an unassailable solution. Now Adam Smith was one of the earliest writers who recognised the social importance of the axiom, that labour is the cause of wealth, and that the permanent occupation of the soil, under intelligible, but under strictly limited conditions, is necessarily antecedent to the economical exhibition of labour.

But the special delusion of Adam Smith's day, and that which he combated with the greatest effect, was the theory of protection. The plea on which the protection of particular industries is defended, is always the public good. Protection, in logical language, is always particular. If everybody were protected, i. e. if every kind of labour were assisted by regulations and restrictions, were sheltered from competition, and provided with a market, it is plain no one would be the better, but every one would be the worse off for the machinery of legislation. Hence universal protection is as gross an absurdity as universal over-production. Nor, for certain reasons, is the protection of particular trades and manufactures any real benefit to those who are engaged in these occupations, except under particular circumstances, and to a limited extent; though the removal of a protection once accorded may be, indeed ordinarily is, accompanied by a loss. It follows, then, that the restriction is the avowed sacrifice of the public to some public object, of which the legislature is conceived to be a better judge than the public can be. It is impossible to state a grosser paradox.

It must not indeed be imagined that the protective system which Adam Smith found in his day had so respectable an origin as a mistaken view of the public good. In the early days of royalty, when the king's prerogative was large and undefined, the monarch assumed the right of licensing individuals in the manufacture of certain goods, or the conduct of certain trades. The grant of such monopolies was freely exercised by Elizabeth. But that prudent princess, when in her later years Parliament remonstrated against these privileged traders, abated her pretensions. Her successor, whose notions of royalty were more extravagant, was forced to abandon the prerogative altogether. But what the King relinquished, the Parliament assumed, and during the seventeenth and eighteenth centuries these privileges of sole trade were freely granted by the legislature.

In order to support the woollen trade, the exportation of wool was made a felony, and when this preposterous punishment was remitted, heavy penalties were still levied on this imaginary offence. The prohibition was continued for many years after the time that not a single ounce of British wool was employed in the manufacture of fine cloth. The legislature investigated the causes which led to the low price of wool, and then discovered that, acting, as always, in the capacity of country gentlemen, they had virtually been engaged in depreciating the value of their own produce. They had taken care previously to ensure the consumption of woollen fabrics by an Act of Parliament, to which I believe no legislation offers a parallel. They did not, perhaps could not, despite their hereditary wisdom, provide that every living person should be decently clad. But they made this provision for the dead. A law declared that every dead body should be buried in a woollen dress, and the officiating clergyman was constrained to certify that the provisions of the law had been obeyed.

A monopoly heightens the profits of an individual. But protection does not, unless the number of persons engaged in the trade or manufacture is limited. The reason for this fact is found in an economical law, that equal capitals, liable to equal risks, are remunerated by equal profits. Hence, if the price of articles is heightened by protection, the competition for producing the high-priced article increases, and profits are equalized. But when the protection is removed, the trade is overstocked; and unless the market is greatly widened, and demand increased, the change is sure to be attended by serious depression. But, as the reputation of English manufactures grew, protection was found to be unnecessary and mischievous, and the mercantile community in this country was the first to claim the benefits of free trade.

The case is somewhat different with agricultural produce. In Adam Smith's time England exported wheat, and the economist thought, with immediate reason, on looking at the circumstances, that the earliest advocates of free trade would be the landowners; the sturdiest remonstrants against it the mercantile community. He was, to a further extent, justified in this impression by the hostile attitude which the merchants assumed against Walpole's scheme of establishing bonded warehouses. But the case was reversed when England ceased to export corn, and the demand for labour increasing, began to depend on foreign supplies. Then it was seen that high rents followed scarcity prices, and the Corn Laws of 1815 were enacted in order to stereotype a scarcity price and its presumed concomitant.

But the violation of an economical law generally bears its own punishment, and that speedily. Any attempt on the part of a legislature to regulate the prices of a foreign product, the same as that which is produced at home, or similar to it, induces violent fluctuations in the price of the home product. As long as the corn laws existed, agricultural distress was a perpetually recurring cry, for nothing induces greater commercial derangement than great variations in the price of products. The farmer was ruined by the machinery which was devised for his benefit. Nor was this the only result. As agriculture is a complex process, the artificial heightening of one among its products is the artificial depression of the rest. And as rent depends on the profit of all products, the landowners reaped no real benefit from protective legislation.

The modern theory of protection as advocated in the United States, in Canada, and in our Australian colonies, is far more subtle and socialistic in its character than the rough-and-ready system of compromises for what are called peculiar burdens, and the concessions to powerful interests which were the real basis of those protective arrangements of ours which lasted up to 1846. The latter were far more open to attack than the former are. They were admitted to serve a purpose of public policy; the sustentation, namely, of an institution which needs hereditary wealth, in order to support hereditary privilege. When interpreted on economical grounds, it was seen that they had no such value as was assigned them; that they did not strengthen, but rather impoverished the social order in whose interests they were enacted. But though this was proved conclusively, and not a few able men among the persons for whose benefit these laws were designed, determined, from an enlightened self-interest, as well as for patriotic reasons, to abandon these guarantees, the English corn laws died hard, and, in the opinion of many critics of political forces, required the accidental calamity of the Irish famine before they could be abrogated. The instincts of large communities are not so much conservative as impassive. They concede to reason long before they act upon the reason which they admit. There is in such societies a wide tract of indifference, between the sympathy which supports, and the antipathy which overthrows customs,—an indifference which ardent partisans underrate, and cynical critics exalt from acquiescence into admiration. There is nothing in the philosophy of politics more hard of interpretation than the question—How far are nations who submit to peculiar institutions prepared, on an emergency, to maintain them?

The Englishman who quits his native country, abandons his social traditions at once and for ever.

No nation of Anglo-Saxon descent has transplanted the institutions of this country to its new home; but almost all these nations or colonies have adopted the theory of protection which Adam Smith assailed. They allege, in defence of this economical heresy, a variety of arguments. Sometimes it is said that the internal revenue can be collected most cheaply by such a process. Sometimes they aver that protection is needed for nascent industries,—a position for which they quote the authority of Mr. Mill. Occasionally they allege a political reason; that it is expedient, apart from economical considerations, to distribute employment as well as to accumulate wealth, and that a nation should be self-sustained. To the last statement there is one answer. It is an axiom which cannot be resisted, that there is no countervailing compensation for the breach of a natural law. No indirect advantage follows on a violation of public policy. In the political, as well as in the moral world, it is impossible to do evil and to succeed in achieving a good, to confer a real benefit by inflicting a real wrong. To the former reasons no answer need be given, for they deserve none. Only this we may say, that protection to nascent industries can never be so great a boon as the ultimate withdrawal of that protection is a certain loss. A permanent protection is no benefit to the protected industry, is a necessary loss to the community at large. A temporary protection is an injury to both parties; to the consumer first, to the producer afterwards. Abundant illustration could be supplied for this position, both in past and present times.

It is more reasonable to refer these enactments, made in the supposed interest of the State, or of inchoate industries, to the incidental compromises of party warfare. Did time permit, it would not be difficult to trace this influence in the protective regulations of the United States and Australia, and to show how much the apology of the present time is an after-thought, a mere explanation, intended to justify the claims of powerful and selfish factions. But as municipal government is a means to an end, that end being the due order of the State, so the imperial policy of an independent community is to be criticised, and, if need be, condemned, if it is seen to be unfriendly to the general good of the human race. Patriotism may be, and has been, the highest public virtue; but it may also be, and more frequently is, a mask for sordid and narrow self-interest. It is the former only when it manifests itself on behalf of the common good of man, or is not at variance with that common good. Treating human nature from its economical aspect, Adam Smith did not discuss municipal or local prosperity, but busied himself with the wealth of nations, with the means, that is to say, by which communities confer mutual benefits.

I do not venture on asserting, as Plato did, that public affairs can be wisely and righteously conducted only when philosophers are rulers, and rulers philosophers, for the dissonance of philosophers is as marked as the discord of parties. There must needs be, when the success of one or other among rival theories involves the undue exaltation or the unfair depression of rival and important interests, a wise, or at least an experienced, arbiter. The wisdom and experience needed are gained for the most part by intelligent reflection on successive failures. The philosophy of government is gathered from the errors of historical administrations; the science of political economy is a host of negative inductions, collected from the fallacies of a mistaken policy. Even were society less apathetic in dealing with these errors and fallacies during their existence and operation, there is wisdom in the slow acceptance of fundamental changes, in the cautious criticism of proposed reformations. Nor is it proper that those who think wisely and carefully should be indignant at the slowness with which their conclusions are accepted. If it be well to labour and succeed, it is even better to labour and be patient. Among the vulgarities of vanity, none is more vulgar than that which cannot say or do what is good and wise, unless the reward of approbation is forthwith and emphatically conceded.

But it cannot be denied that civilisation has been more indebted to what the world calls philosophers and thinkers than it has been to rulers and administrators. The truth is manifest enough when we reflect on the progress which physical analysis and science have effected, and give their weight to the labours of the chemist, the mechanician, the geologist. Not less noteworthy is the influence which the learning of publicists has exercised. The legal reforms of our day had their beginning in the speculative jurisprudence of Bentham and Mackintosh. The doctrine of toleration was first taught by such students as Chillingworth and Locke. The interpretation of those conditions, which guarantee the fullest personal liberty with the greatest administrative vigour, has found no abler exponent than Mr. Mill. But the greatest achievements have been made by the English economists, who have, under great disadvantages, and in the face of strenuous opposition, reversed the policy which was once thought to be the highest, the most undoubted wisdom. It must not be believed that their work is done; that there are no further conquests to be made by this science, whose operations have been so beneficent, though its conclusions often seem harsh and repulsive. But whatever may be done in future, there is no doubt that successive generations of economical reformers will always honour, as the most illustrious of their order, the Scotch Professor who sleeps in the churchyard of the Edinburgh Canongate.

WILLIAM COBBETT.

WILLIAM COBBETT.

IN 1783, everybody thought that the sun of England's glory was for ever set. To those who recognised her reputation in her military greatness, the successful revolt of the American colonies seemed to annihilate her fame. To those who believed, as ninety-nine men in a hundred believed, that the colonial trade, regulated as it was by reciprocal arrangements, was the chief, if not the sole source of England's wealth, the disintegration of the colonial empire was full of sinister omens. To those who believed in the balance of power, as nine hundred and ninety-nine men in a thousand did, it seemed that Great Britain was in danger of occupying a second-rate place in Europe. When Gibbon and Franklin were together in Paris, the latter sought an interview with the former. Gibbon replied that he had the highest respect for Franklin's genius and abilities, but that he could hold no communication with a revolted subject. Franklin replied, that whenever the historian wished to commence a new theme, 'The Decline and Fall of the British Empire,' he would gladly afford him the materials. The retort was at the time believed to be as just as it was severe.

Great Britain recovered herself without difficulty, and ten years afterwards commenced a war, the magnitude and duration of which dwarfed every other contest in which she had been before engaged. At one time she fought with all Europe, as well as with the most indefatigable genius which the art of war has ever developed. She spent sums compared with which her previous outlay had been trifling. She did what she had never done since the days of the Plantagenets, landed an army in a foreign country, and won every pitched battle which she fought, till she had entirely routed her foe, and occupied the territory which she invaded. She annihilated the navy, mercantile as well as armed, of her adversary. She twice dictated terms of peace within the capital of France. Nor did she derive any material advantage from her victory. She paid for all she needed and used. She subsidized her allies, giving high prices for generally worthless service. She came out of this great war too without aggrandising herself. One or two spots in the Mediterranean, and elsewhere, were all her acquisitions, and these she kept, because, according to the judgment of the age, she made Europe secure by these costly stations.

It is not difficult to explain this revival. In the first place, the colonial system was a delusion. The only misfortune was that statesmen did not learn the lesson which the rupture with the American colonies could have taught them. They thanked heaven they had colonies left, and went on tinkering the reciprocal legislation between Canada and the sugar-growing islands on the one hand, and Great Britain on the other. I do not discuss here whether the retention of colonies under the imperial sway is a wise or a mistaken policy; but the whole civilised world has at last learnt, that when two communities agree to trade together exclusively, and prohibit any other than mutual imports, they deliberately make up their minds to lose on both sides. But the fallacy of reciprocity is so inveterate, that, though the government of this country had before it the evidence of a growing trade between Great Britain and the American Union, after the rupture of their political relations, it clung to the reciprocity system till within a few years ago, when it abolished the differential sugar-duties, and later still, rooted out the last fibres of the colonial theory, by remitting the duties on timber.

The means, however, by which Great Britain was enabled to weather the storm, and to ride triumphant out of the far heavier tempest of the twenty-two years' war, were the discovery and utilization of a natural force, and the multiplication of labour by machinery. The strength of Great Britain, from 1780 onwards, lay in the appropriation of the power of steam, and in the marvellous economies of the spinning-jenny and the mule. Compare the cottager's distaff and spindle, the labourer's hammer, the power of man's greatest muscular efforts, with the loom of the modern manufactory, and the vast but manageable force of steam, and you will be able to understand how prodigious are the resources which Watt, Arkwright, and Crompton opened up. It was hardly an extravagant boast, when Arkwright was reported to have said, that if Parliament could continue his patents, he would engage to furnish such ordinary revenue as might be annually necessary for public purposes.

I do not know what are the reasons which have given rise to these late panics about the future industrial position of this country. On economic subjects men are apt to take the easy broad road of abstract reasoning, and to neglect the steep and thorny path of statistical induction. But I have been unable to find out any instance of mechanical genius in any other race but our own, except the solitary discovery of the carding-machine. This, beyond doubt a great invention, though it consists (like all great inventions) in a simple and obvious principle, was discovered by a Frenchman. As some of you are aware, its peculiarity is, that the fibre is delivered over the cylinder, instead of under it. It is said that the discovery was entirely accidental, having been suggested to the inventor by his seeing his daughters brushing their back hair. But I have found no other notable invention for saving human labour which is not the offspring of Anglo-Saxon thought. Other nations can copy, perhaps improve details. The Chinese are perfect in the imitative faculty; Continental machinists have had some success in the management of particulars, a stage beyond Chinese intelligence: but they have hardly entered on the far higher path of invention.

Adam Smith saw and stated clearly why it is that a manufacturing people has far greater strength for enduring the charges of a foreign war than another, the surplus of whose industry consists of what he calls raw produce. The value of manufactured goods consists in the labour which is, so to speak, condensed in them. As they represent greater value in less compass, they are more portable, and more readily permeate into the markets of the world. As they represent greater utility, because they are immediately available for current demand, they are more manageable as articles of sale. As they were at the time, to all intents and purposes, the sole produce of this country, they gave it an exceptional strength. No better example can be found of the power which her manufacturing supremacy gave Great Britain throughout this gigantic struggle than the utter futility of the Berlin and Milan decrees. Napoleon knew well enough that if he could cut off this country from the markets of the Continent, he would seriously cripple her resources. But he miscalculated the strength of his police, as compared with the strength of that which his police was intended to exclude. He built, to be sure, a dyke, but he could not make it impervious to that which he strove to dam out. 'As water flows to the valleys,' says Sanuto, the Venetian merchant of the thirteenth century, 'so traffic forces its way into the channels which thirst for it.' Napoleon's soldiers were clothed in the produce of the Yorkshire and Lancashire looms. His military chests were filled, at enormous sacrifices, from the hoards of British bullion-dealers. The loaf-sugar which he put into his coffee came from Bristol and London, quadrupled in price, because it was imported into France by way of Turkey. To have destroyed the foreign trade of Great Britain, it was necessary to destroy the demands of civilisation, to make society content with the coarse and costly makeshifts of barbarism. I do not deny that British commerce was stunted by the great war, British wealth lessened from what it might have been ; but the resources of other nations were diminished in even greater degree by the constraint which was put upon their demands. Nor do I forget that there came, as there always does come, a reaction from the feverish prosperity of the great war. When nations engage in hostilities, the demand for the labour of those who are not actually fighting becomes urgent : wages are high, profits are high. Everybody seems to thrive. The delusion that they are rendered wealthier by the waste of wealth occupies men's minds, till the inevitable reaction overtakes them. This fallacy possessed our forefathers sixty or seventy years ago, as it possessed our kinsfolk in the American Union four or five years ago. Men mistake feverish energy for real strength, and only learn their error when the fever gives way to exhaustion.

There was, however, one class of persons in this country who never tasted this factitious prosperity. These were the yeomen and the agricultural labourers. Between 1793 and 1815, this country was visited by that series of bad seasons which seems to recur in some undefined cycle. In 1800 and 1801, Great Britain was nearer famine than it had been since the terrible epoch of 1315–1316, when the country was deluged by two years' almost incessant rain. The people could not be relieved from abroad, for the pernicious corn laws—less evil, indeed, than later enactments, but powerful for mischief—shut out the foreign producer. The exceptional sterility of the seasons, and the artificial famine which the law produced, led to various expedients, intended to supply the continual deficiency of food. I remember, when a boy, that my father pointed out to me a field in Hampshire which was cropped for twelve successive years with wheat. Nor were the people ignorant of the causes of their misery. The longing for peace, before the short-lived truce of Amiens, I have learnt from the same authority, was intense and anxious.

The French were not wholly unreasonable in their hatred of Pitt. Before the Revolution broke out, Pitt, a disciple of Adam Smith, was fully persuaded of the necessity of keeping up amicable relations with France. Walpole and he had been the only ministers who possessed even a conception of the true principles of taxation. The former attempted a reform, the establishment of bonded warehouses, in which he failed.

The London merchants, alarmed lest the competition of smaller capitalists should diminish their profits, offered a determined resistance to this measure of good sense, and Walpole was obliged to abandon his project. Pitt was happier, and he made a change which has caused Great Britain to become the *entrepôt* of the world. He proclaimed a policy of peace. He set himself to diminish the public debt, and patronised the scheme of Price's sinking fund. He negotiated a commercial treaty with France, on principles nearly the same as those which Cobden adopted eight years ago. He frankly accepted the situation in America, and strove to cement by friendship the affinity which had been previously that of irritated dependence and ill-judged supremacy. At home he contemplated a Reform Bill, studied the incidence of taxation, and resolved on revising the system of national finance. He was courageous as well as powerful; confident in his own resources and popular with his countrymen. He was, it is true, opposed, but the opposition to which he was subjected merely urged him to greater efforts, was the healthy stimulus to a vigorous mind.

Again, Pitt loved freedom. He reformed the law of libel against the licence of ministerial prosecutors, too soon, indeed, to return to those measures of repression in which he was finally outdone by Sidmouth and Castlereagh, men who copied the worse parts of Pitt's nature, as Vansittart parodied the desperate measures of Pitt's later finance. He constantly and energetically opposed the slave trade, even after he had retrograded from his earlier sympathies with public liberty. It is possible that the real reason which induced him to consent to the trial of Hastings was his detestation of the cruelties which that satrap committed, though he has been charged, on insufficient grounds as it seems to me, with meaner motives. It is certain that he denounced the Black Acts of the West India statute book, and believed that cruelty and vindictiveness in dealing with subject races were neither policy nor justice. Wilberforce, that strange mixture of prejudice and benevolence, of piety and policy, was on thoroughly good terms with him, and Wilberforce would not have honoured a man without a heart.

But the vigour and virtue of Pitt's heart and nature were not proof against panic, though he resisted the panic to which he ultimately succumbed for more than two years. In 1789, the Constituent Assembly, summoned by Louis XVI, met in Paris. There was abundant need, urgent need, for sweeping reform, and it cannot be denied that the Assembly went to it with a will. They abolished primogeniture, which, by the way, never prevailed in France to the extent which English custom has sanctioned; they made taxation equal; they annulled feudal privileges, gave liberty of religious worship, took away the power of arbitrary arrest, granted universal suffrage, made the administration of justice public, and appropriated Church-lands to secular purposes. The condition of France was desperate, and the remedies were searching and drastic.

A year after the meeting of this Assembly, Burke published his 'Reflections on the French Revolution.' Never did any book produce such an effect. To be sure, it was as the torch to gunpowder. The Court, the Aristocracy, and the Clergy were immeasurably alarmed at the progress of the Revolution. There was some reason for their fears. King George was a respectable man, whose private virtues made his political traits, namely, inflexible obstinacy, joined to absolute unscrupulousness as to the means by which his end should be aimed at, more mischievous than the vices of his children. His eldest son was a monster of meanness and profligacy; nor were the rest of the Royal family much better. One instance will suffice. The Horse Guards, always liable to sinister influences, were under the dominion of Mrs. Clarke and Nancy Parsons.

The Peerage of the day was as worthless. The right of hereditary legislation was conferred on those who were able to return members for rotten boroughs. The Lowther of the time was made Earl of Lonsdale, for the sufficient reason that he controlled the representation of Cumberland and Westmorland, and their boroughs. How the Lowther had gained his influence is shown in the history of Wordsworth's family. The English aristocracy grew rich upon pensions and sinecures. Pitt, who was personally pure, suffered this to go on freely. Mr. Goldwin

Smith has adduced numerous instances of this form of peculation. A little pains would supply as many more examples.

Still more flagitious, however, was the conduct of the prelates. This was the age of those ecclesiastical cormorants, Tomline, Cornwallis, Moore. These men were as negligent of their duties, as they were rapacious after preferment. Never, perhaps, in the whole course of English history, was the English establishment so debased. There was some life in the Evangelical clergy, who were then discredited and persecuted. The Dissenters, though tolerated, were politically powerless, and had to a great extent fallen from their austere rule. The followers of Wesley were poor; those of Whitfield few, and without influence. Underneath this hierarchy lay a profoundly ignorant people. The Church and King mobs, the populace which could be stirred by fanatics, were found in the great towns,—such mobs as those who were roused by Lord George Gordon in London, and which sacked Priestley's house in Birmingham. Society was composed of scum and dregs. In those days it was easy to commit the worst of political crimes; to enlist ignorance on behalf of injustice, to stimulate the sordid passions of one class in order that the sordid interests of another class might be protected and continued.

This Burke did, unconsciously or wilfully. Some persons have tried to explain the Beaconsfield reflections by the hypothesis that the author had suddenly gone mad. If a morbid egotism makes men mad, Burke was always mad. If sudden and ardent sympathy for any cause which is suffering, whatever its previous demerits were, is generosity, Burke was always generous. As there are men who always side with the stronger, so there is an impulse, rarer indeed, but more attractive, which induces other minds to side with the weaker party. It is probable that Burke knew nothing of the social state of France before the Revolution. It is certain that any man of sense would have acknowledged the evils which it contained, and the difficulties which surrounded the employment of remedies. It is still more certain that had it not been for the excesses which followed on the declaration of Pilnitz and the manifesto of the Duke of Brunswick, Burke's declamatory invective would have had no lasting reputation, beyond that of its vigorous style, and the characteristic sincerity of its hyperbole.

Burke's known love of justice and hatred of oppression assisted the intrinsic force of the work that he published. It was known that he had been a Liberal, a keen lover of his country, a generous friend to subject and wronged races. Viewed in the magic mirror which he put before the public, Louis XVI became, instead of a dull, well-meaning man, the chief business of whose life was that of repairing clocks and watches, a wise and judicious benefactor of his country, against whose prudent concessions a host of mad fanatics were striving;—the Queen, instead of being a frivolous intriguing woman (to whom suffering taught such dignity and fortitude, that she afterwards became almost sublime), was spoken of as a radiant angel, who challenged the worship of all true and loyal hearts;—the worthless nobles, and yet more worthless clergy of France, were noble cavaliers, and exemplary ministers of Christ. The Stuarts were bad enough, but they never bred a monster like Philip Egalité. The Church of Tomline and Cornwallis was sordid enough, but it failed to produce such a wretch as Talleyrand, bishop of Autun, who fled from the diocese he disgraced when danger was near, took the pay of the Directory as a spy in the United States, and was a traitor to every constitution and every ruler which France had. The English nobles during the days of Sandwich, Chesterfield, Thurlow, were licentious and heartless enough, but they were whole periods of development superior to the satyrs who thronged the French court. The peasantry of England were ignorant and debased enough, but they were civilised by the side of those hordes of savages whom the customs of the French monarchy had degraded, and the energies of the French Revolution, stimulated by the atrocious proclamation of the Duke of Brunswick, ultimately let loose upon mankind.

I know of but one period in modern history in which a similar delusion, had it occupied a mind like that of Burke, and had it found utterance in the words of so great a master of rhetoric, might have produced equal evils. Seven years ago, there were men—good and otherwise prudent men—who defended the social system of the slave-holding States in the American Union, who spoke about the chivalry of the South, and, ignoring the mean whites, lauded the patriarchal relations of the master and the slave. The same kind of reasoning, the same misstatement of facts, the same ignorance existed in this country as made it possible for a defence of the Southern policy to appear respectable. Fortunately there was no Burke, and still more fortunately, had there been a Burke, the public was better informed. Even yet more fortunately there was no congress at Pilnitz, and no Duke of Brunswick, and no Directory liberated from slavery, and suffered to run riot, under the joint influence of new-found licence and ferocious panic. But there was a Pitt, though most fortunately he was not exposed to the same temptations, and therefore did not commit himself to the same reaction.

For more than two years Pitt abstained from meddling in continental affairs, and therefore was resisting the anti-Gallican tendencies of the party whose interests he administered. He had every reason to do so, for he sincerely desired peace and economy, if for no higher reason, at least for this, that he longed to give his financial reforms a fair trial. No writer has illustrated this period of history more lucidly than Cobden, whose pamphlet ' 1793 and 1853,' must needs be studied by all who pretend to form an impartial judgment on the question. Pitt, I am persuaded, strove against the current with all his might.

In the year 1792 he proposed reduced estimates for the military expenditure of the country, and all went well till the battle of Jemappes and the occupation of the Austrian Netherlands and Savoy.

Nor can there be, I think, a doubt of the motive which finally drove Pitt into this reactionary career, —a motive which Lord Brougham has stated with his usual clearness. Pitt was joined by the aristocratic Whigs, and was so far strengthened in Parliament. Had he, however, united with Fox, he might have baffled the war party. To have done so, however, would have compelled him to share his power with a rival, to have divided his reputation with a political enemy. So he preferred war to peace, ambition to his country's good, supremacy to magnanimity. Representing as he did in Parliament the faction which longed for war, which profited by it, and which was, under the unreformed Parliament, almost in possession of the nation, (for in that day, according to Mr. Grey, 154 persons sent 307 members to Parliament,) he took a step from which retreat was impossible, he declared a war which could not and did not cease without dishonour, as long as Napoleon was victorious in Europe. Nor did the miseries of that era cease with the Battle of Waterloo. They continued for seventeen years afterwards, till the grant of Parliamentary Reform.

Those who commit themselves to reaction in politics, just as those who are renegades or converts in religion, rarely go half lengths. Strafford is a noteworthy illustration of this rule, by the greatness of his apostasy, and by the severity with which that apostasy was punished. Pitt was no exception. He permitted a Reign of Terror in Ireland, hardly less atrocious, though better concealed than the massacres of September, and the fusillade at Lyons. He permitted the reign of Dundas in Scotland, and revived, in part at least, the memories of the Stuart times of Claverhouse and Dalziel in Edinburgh. The country swarmed with spies and informers. When ministers pay for secret intelligence against their countrymen, and rulers smother the past in acts of indemnity, they are self-condemned. Sidmouth and Castlereagh continued what Pitt began, but by viler means, and with viler tools. It may be doubted whether Oates and Turberville were baser than Castles, Oliver, and Edwards. Sometimes indeed Pitt was defied and repulsed. In 1796 he prosecuted Horne Tooke in vain, for a Westminster jury acquitted him. Addington contrived afterwards to visit the grave offence of escaping a government prosecution by laying a penalty on the culprit and on the order to which he belonged. Horne Tooke was a clergyman, and we owe the law by which the clergy are excluded from the House of Commons, to the baffled rage of Pitt's partisans. Habeas Corpus was suspended, the press was gagged, and the assault on public liberty which this minister perpetrated, had (according to Mr. Massey, the very reverse of a Jacobin in politics) no parallel since the worst times of the most tyrannical monarchs. In order to put down a spirit of revolution in France, the United Kingdom ran the risk of a counter-revolution, in which every liberty she had gained from the days of the Great Charter was in peril.

I have given this rough and imperfect, but I hope just sketch of the social and political history of the time; a sketch the outlines of which are taken as much from Alison and Scott, as from Massey and Cobden; because, as I stated in a previous lecture, it is impossible to study political economy with profit unless one combines with it the philosophy and the facts of history, and gains an insight into social life. One part of political economy, I repeat, that, namely, which deals with the causes and conditions under which wealth may be produced, is scientific in the highest sense, and may be studied, but not studied well, apart from illustrations. But every other exposition of the subject is hollow and unreal, unless it takes note of such facts as those which I have recounted.

William Cobbett was born on March 9, 1762. His father was a small farmer who lived at Farnham, in Surrey. His grandfather was a day-labourer, who worked from his marriage till his death—which occurred a year before Cobbett's birth—on the same farm. Beyond this, he did not trace his pedigree, or did not care to do so. His father seems to have obtained an education superior to that which generally fell to the lot of the sons of agricultural labourers.

He thus raised himself a little in life. He had arithmetic enough to be a land-measurer, and in these days of irregular fields, and piece-work in harvest, the services of such a person were constantly in requisition. So he prospered in his little way, for he farmed a small tract of land on the verge of the most fertile valley in the South, where the soil is twenty feet deep, and the hop, our English vine, grows luxuriantly, and fills the air in early autumn with its fragrance. Here this peasant farmer brought up his four sons, taught them such simple learning as he knew, and boasted that his boys, the eldest only fifteen years old, could do as much honest work as any four men in the parish. Here, too, Cobbett learned his power of describing rural life,—a power which no poet has rivalled, a power which he retained in all its freshness to the last day of his life.

A little below the Thames, at Weybridge, there commences a tract of moorland, broken by the upper range of chalk downs at Guildford; but continuing, in varying breadth, till it reaches the lower range of chalk downs above Portsmouth. This range of heather, extending through Surrey, and the borders of Hampshire and Sussex, contains alternately tracts of barren sand and gravel, and valleys of surpassing richness. One of these valleys is Farnham, the rich soil of which is sharply bounded by the unfruitful sands of Aldershot and Frensham. In this contrast of desert and garden Cobbett learned his love of rural life. Here he cultivated his keen sense of natural beauty, and stored his memory with those pictures of rude and cultivated scenery which he drew with such fidelity in his shop at Philadelphia, New York, or Pall Mall; in his farmhouse at Botley, and in his prison of Newgate. The soft outline of the downs, the wide expanse of the heather, the flow of the clear streams, the shade of the lanes, worn down deep into the sand and gravel by the waggons which had passed through them for centuries, the hazel coppices, stunted on the south-west by the Atlantic winds where exposed, or thriving luxuriantly in sheltered places, the finches, the nightingales, in summer, the fieldfares and plover in winter, the heavily-laden orchards and brown cornfields were always before his ear or eye. He was a farmer when a politician; and throughout the hot and bitter struggle of his life, there were two kinds of Englishmen whom he always loved and laboured for, the farmer and the farm-labourer; the former not yet swollen into his present pretensions, the latter not yet dwarfed into his terrible degradation.

In these primeval times, from which a real epoch separates us now, the well-to-do yeoman hired most of his hinds by the year, boarded and lodged them in his home, and sat at the head of his table when they dropped in at noon from their work to their dinner. The homestead contained its large low room on the ground-floor, with its spacious chimney and long bacon-rack, with the parlour door at one corner of the great kitchen. This parlour was the mistress' sanctum, with its corner cupboards and treasures of old spoons and older china. Below the yeoman in wealth, but not much below him in station and plenty, were the married labourers, most of whom cultivated some land of their own,—cottage garden or small field by their houses; and who, in the general occupations of the farm, were employed all the year through on varied work. Abject penury was wellnigh unknown; the terrible canker of pauperism had not yet eaten out the better part of the agricultural labourer's nature.

Cobbett rose, under singular difficulties, many of which were of his own creation, from the condition of a farmer's boy to that of a member of the British Parliament. When a child of thirteen years old he ran away to Windsor, and got employment in the king's garden there. Even here he began that self-education of his in hard coarse humour; for he tells us that he spent his last threepence in buying Swift's 'Tale of a Tub,' and that when he lost the book at sea years afterwards, he felt the loss more acutely than he ever did far greater calamities. He returned home, and when he was seventeen he was led by a sudden impulse to run away again. This time he went to London, and when his funds were nearly exhausted, got a place as a lawyer's clerk. Then he tried to go to sea, but was rejected, humanely, it seems, by the captain of the flag-ship at Portsmouth. At last, just at the close of the American War of

Independence, he enlisted in a regiment which was recruiting for Nova Scotia. In a short time his diligence, shrewdness, and punctuality were rewarded. Within a twelvemonth he was raised to the rank of serjeant-major, and was able to make considerable savings from his pay. In 1791 he obtained his discharge, receiving, at the same time, a high testimonial to character from his colonel, who afterwards obtained an unhappy eminence in connection with the Irish outbreak of 1798, for the colonel was Lord Edward Fitzgerald. After his discharge he married.

Cobbett's marriage was eminently characteristic. When he was in New Brunswick, he saw, on an early December morning, a girl, not more than thirteen years of age, scrubbing a washtub in the snow. She was the daughter of a soldier, a serjeant-major like Cobbett himself. He resolved to marry her in due time. It seems that his project was favoured by the girl's father. Three or four years after he made this resolve, the parents of the girl were ordered back to Woolwich. Cobbett, thinking the risks of a residence in this town were neither few nor slight, recommended her to take up her residence with some decent people who would board her; and to meet this expense he handed her over all his savings, amounting to 150 guineas. They then parted for three or four years. When he returned to England, he found her engaged as a maid-of-all-work in a family. She returned him his 150 guineas unbroken, and in a few weeks they were married. In the spring of 1792, Cobbett went to France, and applied himself diligently to learning French. Fearing the turn which the Revolution was likely to take, he quitted the country and sailed to America, appearing at Philadelphia in October.

At first Cobbett maintained himself by teaching English to the French emigrants. In the early days of the French Revolution there was a close and friendly intercourse between the Americans and the French. The feeling was natural; for the latter had served the former at a very opportune time, by declaring war against Great Britain during the crisis of the revolutionary war. This intimacy was closest between the Democratic party in America,—the party of Jefferson, Madison, and Monroe,—and the French. The Federal party, the heads of which were Washington, Adams, and Hamilton, were rather disposed to cultivate the friendship of Great Britain. The latter were on the whole in the ascendant, and had, in the reformation of 1787, given larger powers to Congress, besides handing over the executive, under certain checks and guarantees, to the President. But the contest of parties was exceedingly bitter. Such a man as Cobbett immediately felt himself in his element. According to his own account, which there seems no reason to doubt, overtures had been made to him by Talleyrand, who was then filling the congenial office of agent and spy in the United States, under the cloak of a general dealer in New York. Cobbett rejected his advances. He had determined, as soon as possible, to attack the Democrats. How violently hostile they were to England, is suggested by the whimsical project of Thornton, who proposed that the language, since it could not be abandoned, should be put into masquerade, by spelling all words phonetically, and by printing the letters upside down.

Cobbett began his partisanship with a defence of Washington's treaty of amity and commerce with Great Britain. With him political writing was necessarily personal; so he assailed Priestley, Tom Paine, and Franklin, with a bitterness as novel as it was pungent, under the thin disguise of his favourite *nom de plume*, Peter Porcupine. He soon raised himself a host of enemies, as well as a circle of admirers. Some of the former took to traducing his character, and to circulating damaging statements about his previous career. To these libels he answered by giving the world a brief autobiography, into which, full as it is of that peculiar rural description of which he was so great a master, various passages of singular pungency are inserted. One of these passages, in which the writer glances at Franklin, may serve as a specimen of Cobbett's style. He has been giving an account of his ancestry, which he is able to trace no further back than to his grandfather.

'Every one will, I hope, have the goodness to believe that my grandfather was no philosopher. Indeed he was not. He never made a lightning rod, nor bottled up a quart of sunshine in his life. He was no almanack maker, nor quack, nor chimney-doctor, nor soap boiler, nor ambassador, nor printer's devil.

Neither was he a deist; and all his children were born in wedlock. The legacies he left were his scythe, his reap-hook, and his flail. He bequeathed no old and irrecoverable debts to an hospital. He never cheated the poor during his life, nor mocked them at his death. He has, it is true, been suffered to sleep quietly beneath the green sward; but if his descendants cannot point to his statue over the door of a library, they have not the mortification to hear him daily accused of having been a profligate, a hypocrite, and an infidel.' In this kind of hitting, Cobbett had hardly a rival, and certainly no superior. It is not marvellous, therefore, that, unable to cope with him in the use of the pen, his numerous enemies tried to crush him by other expedients,—by threats, by prosecutions, and by violence. Meanwhile he continued to increase the hatred felt towards him by acts of singular audacity.

He opened a shop at Philadelphia, and, by way of showing his daring, he filled his windows with portraits of George the Third and his ministers, of nobles and prelates. He denounced the Revolution in France, and the acts of the Convention, with as much savage bitterness as that with which any man might have reprobated the deeds of the Committee of Public Safety. He scoffed in unmeasured terms at the independence of the United States. He ridiculed the Constitution of the Union, and predicted the inconveniences which would ensue from its written and therefore inelastic forms. He held up to contempt the doctrine on which the Americans prided themselves, the democratic equality of all men, under a fable, the coarse humour of which has never been equalled. He compared society to the various vessels in a crockery-shop, and the republic in which he was living to the same vessels rendered uniformly worthless by being shattered into fragments of uniform value. But his bitterest scorn was reserved for English sympathisers with American institutions. He received threatening letters. These he published in his journal. He added comments on them, not intended so much to sting the writers, for whom he cared nothing, as to hold up those institutions to obloquy which, he assumed, could alone produce such correspondents.

Cobbett could hardly have been unaware that a fiftieth part of the political libels which he uttered in the United States would have been sufficient, in his native country, to bring down on his head the merciless penalties of Pitt's gagging acts. He railed at transatlantic liberty with all the licence which that liberty allowed, with greater virulence than any other community has ever permitted. But it has constantly been seen that the fiercest enemies of popular liberty have always invoked and used the freedom which they assail. The men who after the Revolution would have coerced the press, uttered the most malignant libels against the Government which permitted free speech. Had Swift written a tithe of the calumnies against the favourites of James, which he published against the Whigs of the junto and the Irish administration of Walpole, he would have been put in the pillory, and been whipped at the cart's tail, as Oates was. Not that we need wonder or complain at this. When base and servile natures are emancipated against their will, they always at first abuse the benefits which are conferred on them. In this way, and in this way only, can they be schooled into the dignity and truthfulness of real freedom. Cobbett, it is true, was never servile, and seldom base, but he was intoxicated with the freedom of the institutions which he attacked. Had he been left alone, he would, without doubt, have exhausted his petulance.

I said before that Burke, from innate generosity, always sided with the weaker party. Cobbett followed the same course, from an innate spirit of contention. The selfwill of his youth, strong and resolute beyond parallel, had raised him from the condition of a farmer's boy to that of a powerful writer. When he was little more than thirty years old, he had gained a name in both hemispheres—a far more arduous task than at present. He had but little knowledge of books, and even less of other men's thoughts. But he had a memory of singular retentiveness, a keen eye, an instant appreciation of the ludicrous, a marvellous mastery over the English tongue, and a unique faculty of inventing suggestive nicknames which stuck like birdlime. Added to these mental powers was an almost unique egotism. Some egotists become morbid; but Cobbett's egotism was always healthy. Some become ridiculous; but Cobbett's humour saved him from this risk. 'I wrote for fame,' he says, 'and was urged forward by illtreatment.' He never lost sight of the fame he sought for, and he never forgot the illtreatment which he endured. Once, and once only, he made himself ridiculous. When he returned from his second journey to America, he brought back Paine's bones, and advertised gold rings, each to contain a lock of that notorious republican's hair. His motion, when he got into the House of Commons, that the King should be petitioned to strike off Peel's name from the list of the Privy Council, was the act of a man who is ignorant of his fellow-men, and mistakes his own hatreds for popular opinions. He gave the clue to this ignorance of other minds than his own, when he refused the Speaker's invitation on the plea that he was unused to the society of gentlemen. His egotism would not allow him to defer to any man, in any place or in any company. The Speaker thought he was modest. He knew little of his man.

The persecution which Cobbett underwent in the United States was a series of prosecutions for libel. Like most of these prosecutions, they were unfair, or at best a cloak for procedure against a man notoriously unpopular, who must be crushed, no matter how. Cobbett had unluckily, too, made an enemy of the chief justice of the State; and in those days a judge was no mean foe when he nourished a grudge against prisoner or defendant, prosecutor or plaintiff. Not indeed that the judge in the city of Brotherly Love was harsher or more unfair than Braxfield on the Scotch, or Erskine on the English bench; that Erskine whom Cobbett, in later days, delighted to designate by his second title of Clackmannan.

The first prosecution which Cobbett defended, (and he almost invariably conducted his defence in person,) was that on account of a libel against the King of Spain. It was certain that such a prosecution would fail, and it failed. But in the next case his enemies were more fortunate.

A certain Dr. Rush had advertised a new cure for yellow fever. It consisted in copious bleedings and in prodigious doses of calomel. The doctor puffed his remedies, and Cobbett, eager for attack, assailed him, called him Sangrado, and published in his paper parallel passages from the physician's method of treatment, and Sangrado's conversations with Gil Blas. Rush prosecuted him, and laid his damages at 500 dollars. It seems that Cobbett foresaw the result of the trial, for he migrated to New York, declaring that while his old enemy was in power and office, the issue could not be fairly tested. He was right, for the jury assessed Rush's damages at 5000 dollars. But Cobbett, after all, vindicated his criticism on Rush, for Washington fell a victim to the treatment of the Doctor. In New York, Cobbett published a new paper, under the name of 'The Rushlight,' in which he reiterated his libels on his medical foe, and after a short time came back to England.

With the exception of a few weeks, Cobbett had been absent from England for sixteen years. No contrast could be more marked than that of his social position at his departure and at his return. He left his country a common soldier, he returned to it one of the most powerful political writers in the world, the courageous advocate of English institutions, of constitutional monarchy, of Church and State, under the most untoward circumstances, in the face of the bitterest and most implacable enemies of the old country. He was immediately adopted by some of the anti-revolutionary Whigs, such as Wyndham. He took a shop in Pall Mall, and commenced his career as a journalist and publicist. Pitt, however, refused to meet him, and, as he never forgave a slight, he speedily found opportunities of resenting this act of contempt.

It is not, I think, difficult to explain Pitt's indifference to a man who might have been, under judicious management, so powerful an ally. The Prime Minister was absolute in the House of Commons, so absolute, that people believed his resignation, the year following, was a mere act of dissimulation, intended to save his reputation for liberality in dealing with the Catholic claims, and for consistency in negotiating the short-lived and shameful Peace of Amiens. But Pitt cared little for the press. He cared, it seems, in the height of his power, but little for votes. He held his followers together by offices and pensions, his party by dread of revolutionary France. He brought Canning into Parliament. But for a short time Canning was well-disposed to the party of Fox. When he saw that he could get nothing except by the active support of his patron, he abandoned his predilections, and falsified Sheridan's prediction. This sudden conversion of a young man, afterwards famous for lampoons, made him the object of an epigram at the time :—

> 'The turning of coats is so commonly known,
>   That no one would think to attack it;
> But no case until now was so flagrantly shown
>   Of a schoolboy in turning his jacket.'

But how could the author of the Gagging Acts, of the Press prosecutions, of the Act of Indemnity, patronize a journalist?

Cobbett revenged himself by going over to the party of Burdett, Cartwright, and Hunt, by sneering in characteristic fashion at Pitt's expedients and policy, and in particular by holding up the King's family to contempt. His weekly 'Political Register' was commenced in 1802; and was continued, with few interruptions, till his death. But he still retained his hatred for revolutionary France, declined to illuminate his shop after the Peace of Amiens, and bore the smashing of his windows with his customary courage, having taken the precaution of getting his wife and children out of the way of danger.

Politicians in the beginning of the present century, when the laws were administered by men like Kenyon, wrote with the sword of Damocles hanging over them. If one is astonished at their courage, one is amazed at their virulence. Press prosecutions, however energetically conducted by governments, are invariably failures as part of the machinery for repressing opinion, except perhaps when they are conducted by an agency like the Spanish Inquisition. We need not go to our neighbours across the Channel for proofs of this position, for illustrations of the way in which inuendos, which cannot be grasped by the hand of the law, are far more damaging than downright open speech, free criticism. Despotic governments have silenced plain comments on their acts, only to suggest the more subtle attacks of fable, parable, apologue, or tale. The satires of Juvenal are far bitterer than the philosophic romance of Tacitus. The gross apologue of Rabelais is more biting than the diatribes of Luther. You may find political satire in plenty in the fables of La Fontaine, and in the fairy tales of Hans Andersen.

In Cobbett's time the press was violently personal. A publication, in which Hunt and Cartwright were probably interested, called 'The Black Dwarf,' lavished weekly abuse of the coarsest kind on the public men of the day. These papers circulated by thousands, and were read with the greatest avidity. But no papers were more popular than the 'Porcupine,' the 'Register,' the 'Twopenny Trash,' and the

'Gridiron.' I have said that Cobbett was an adept in the art of suggestive nicknames. Such were Prosperity Robinson, Old Glory Burdett. In his later years he similarly vilified the two clergymen who promulgated and adopted the theory of population, Malthus and Mr. Lowe of Bingham, the latter the well-known father of a more distinguished son. He had an equal aversion to a living economist of great eminence in poor-law and sanitary reform, Mr. Edwin Chadwick, whom he always designated as Penny-a-line Chadwick.

'The best remedy for the evils of liberty,' says a great and wise philosopher of our own time, 'is more liberty.' Never was this adage more exactly verified than in the history of the political press. When the law of libel was relaxed, when the repeal of the infamous Six Acts of Sidmouth heralded further concessions to the right of free comment on public affairs, the tone of the anonymous press continually improved. As more liberty was given, less licence was taken. It is not too much, I think, to say, that whatever are the evils of anonymous writing, (and it is a moot question whether it has done more good than mischief,) its evils were vastly greater under the repressive system of fifty years ago. It is sometimes said that statesmen should not yield to clamour, to sentimental grievances, to popular demand. It is a truer interpretation of the function of a statesman that he should face, on just principles, clamour, grievance, demand; and should silence, satisfy, concede each, if needs must, by wise and equitable legislation. This is the canon of true progress. For the art of the statesman is like that of the physician. It takes no action when the body is sound, it treats that disease only which it knows by symptoms. Fifty years ago men thought it wisdom to meet the disease by driving in the eruption. But experience teaches, as its best learning, that what was once thought wisdom, has been found folly.

In 1800, Cobbett was prosecuted for a political libel on Lord Hardwick and Lord Plunket. He was cast in damages to the amount of £500. But a further prosecution in 1810 ruined and finally embittered him. Certain militiamen at Ely had been guilty of some act of insubordination. For this offence, five of the ringleaders were flogged. The punishment, according to the brutal fashion of the time, was severe. But the sting in Cobbett's mind consisted in the fact that the 500 lashes inflicted on each of these offenders was superintended by a guard of the Hanoverian legion, then quartered in England. Cobbett's wrath was roused, and he poured his whole fury on the Administration. He was prosecuted, sentenced to two years' imprisonment in Newgate, to a fine of £1000 to the King, and was ordered to find securities for good behaviour in a large amount. The sentence was probably intended to be fatal. Cobbett was passionately fond of his farm at Botley, and lived as much as he could in the open air. He loved his family, his wife and children, as men who hate earnestly love earnestly. He has left on record that he never uttered but once a harsh word to wife or child, and that he bitterly repented of that one harsh word spoken to one child. He was sentenced to two years' imprisonment in a filthy gaol, in the filthiest part of London.

He bore up, however, bravely. He wrote with unabated vigour, and directed the farm at Botley with untiring interest. Once, it seems, he tried to make terms. One Reeves gave in evidence, ten years after Cobbett's conviction, that the prisoner offered to stop his 'Register' if he were released. His political enemies chuckled over this offer and refused it. So Cobbett continued his 'Register,' and served out the term of his imprisonment. 'The Regent,' says Cobbett, 'got the £1000, and no doubt held it in trust for his father.'

On his release he was entertained at a dinner given by Burdett. When the guests lifted their soup-plates, each found the reprint of a lampoon which, some years before, Cobbett had written on his host, and which some waiter had been bribed to distribute. I heard this story from an uncle of mine, who was present at the banquet. The trick failed, however, to produce more than a momentary discomposure. Men who were political prisoners in Newgate fifty years ago got bronzed and ready in emergencies. Afterwards, Cobbett wrote more lampoons on Burdett.

In 1817, Sidmouth passed the Six Acts, the object of which was to further restrain the political press. Cobbett fled to the United States, and lived for two years on Long Island, writing his 'Register' as usual. He averred that he fled to avoid the Six Acts. But he was also in debt to the amount of £30,000. When in America, he wrote his English Grammar, and, with characteristic pungency, made his illustrations the vehicle of political jibes. In 1819 he returned, with Paine's bones. He was again prosecuted, now by a private person, was cast in damages to the amount of £1000; Scarlett, with the keen enjoyment of a renegade, leading against him. He turned butcher, and soon became bankrupt.

He stood for Coventry, and again for Preston, his rival at the latter place being the present Lord Derby. In 1830, aided by the interest of Mr. Fielden, he was returned for Oldham, and sat for that borough till his death in June, 1835. He made no way in the House of Commons, but rather damaged his reputation. He was buried in the graveyard of his native town. As a boy, I remember the circumstances of his funeral, and the attendance with which the farmer's son was gathered to the grave of his forefathers. Elliott, the Corn-law rhymer, who had, in the smoky streets and wild moors of Lancashire, felt the keenest relish for

Cobbett's descriptions of the warm, rich, sunny valleys of Surrey, sung of him—

> 'And in some little lone churchyard,
>   Beside the growing corn,
> Lay gentle nature's stern prose bard—
>   Her mightiest peasant-born.'

As a political writer Cobbett, who occupied a first place in the criticism of current politics for more than forty years, had few rivals. He was a great master of that homely, idiomatic English, which is persuasive by its very plainness and lack of ornament, and which is exhibited in its perfection by another farmer's son—another politician, but also a statesman of the highest and noblest type. A fortnight before Cobbett's death Cobden published his first political work, under the title of 'England, Ireland, and America,' and in it, using such English as Cobbett used, announced a policy which is now become identical, on the acknowledgment of all parties, with prudence and good sense.

As a controversialist, Cobbett was constantly unfair from his vindictive violence. Men who have been persecuted are rarely tolerant; the most patient martyr has often been the most savage inquisitor. Cobbett felt himself wounded, and he retaliated with ferocious energy. 'He had,' says Hazlitt, 'the back trick simply the best of any man in Illyria.' He never hesitated in his revenge, and he continued it after revenge was indecent, as well as superfluous. He hated Castlereagh—most of Castlereagh's opponents had reason to hate him—during his life, and he gloated over the circumstances of Castlereagh's suicide after his death. Canning felt the blows of his bludgeon; for Canning, like most satirists, was sensitive. Lord Lytton calls Cobbett 'the contentious man;' but the adjective, though eminently suggestive, hardly covers the range of this writer's controversial nature. He was vindictive, with the greatest facility of retaliation. Some men, like Wilkes, are irresistible in repartee; others, like Canning, have a vein of polished irony; some, like Moore, have a gay wit, which pleases even when it stings the most, and is hardly offensive to its object: but Cobbett was capable of that harsh ridicule which springs from an unforgiving nature, and is unforgiven;—which bruises instead of wounding; but which roused in its day whole masses of the people to band themselves against what they were taught to believe was wrong or selfishness.

It may seem to most of my hearers that the politician is more prominent in Cobbett than the economist. I have, it is to be admitted, given greater prominence to the former constituent in the career of this remarkable man; but, in truth, the substratum of all Cobbett's positive convictions was economical. He never swerved from his purpose,— that of undertaking the defence of the farmer and the peasant. As a consequence, his influence was exceedingly great among the class from whom he sprung.

He denounced, not wisely indeed (for he had little tincture of scientific method), the Corn Laws. He saw that the object which the framers of these famous statutes had, was to keep up rents, to stereotype the price of food, and to do this, not necessarily to the profit of the farmer, but certainly to the injury of the peasant. He knew that high prices of food do not imply high prices of labour, and he dreaded the degradation of the English peasant to the level of the Irish cottier. His hatred of the potato, as an article of food, nearly equalled his hatred of Castlereagh and Sidmouth. He predicted the Irish famine as the inevitable consequence of using the accursed root, as he called it, on which the Irish lived. When Brougham, in the ardour of his educational reforms, was predicting that the time would come in which the English peasant would be familiar with Locke and Bacon, Cobbett retorted that he was far more anxious for the time in which the peasant would not need to put a lock on his bacon.

But Cobbett could not, or would not, point out that the corn laws were as suicidal as they were unjust. He did not show that a farmer's trade was multiform, that if he grew corn, he also bred and kept stock, and that if an artificial price was put on the former, the value of the latter would be certainly depreciated. The corn laws went further. They stimulated the production of one kind of grain only, and so lowered the price of the rest. Had he reflected on the economical circumstances which attended the selfish folly of the corn laws, and had he brought to bear his vigorous good sense on the project, he might have obviated, in great measure at least, the hateful system which Cobden overthrew. He had such influence with the tenant farmers, that he might have banded them together against the legislation which affected to be in their interests, but which mocked them with the hopes of an unattainable advantage.

In one of his latest works he tells us, that, at Charlbury in Oxfordshire, every man who had been a farmer thirty years before, was on the poor-book in 1835. He witnessed, with wondering indignation, the gradual decline of the class which he loved, and to which he belonged by birth. He did not, however, see how distinctly traceable this fact was to the system of precarious tenure, of artificial legislation, and thereupon of perpetual and damaging fluctuations in the price of the agricultural staple. It may be the case, as some economists think, that the large system of cultivation is better suited to the conditions under which high farming is carried on, than small cultivation can be. The hypothesis is at least doubtful. But there is no doubt that this large system has destroyed the yeomanry and degraded the peasantry of England. It is equally certain that the change has not been induced as a consequence of the economical principles with which it is supposed to be in harmony, but in absolute defiance of them.

The condition of the peasant is now lower than

it was even in Cobbett's time. In the days of Arthur Young, the agricultural labourer was far better off than he is now. You who live in the centre of active industries, and among whom, therefore, the rate of wages in rural districts is heightened by the competition of manufacturing energy, have probably no conception of the stolid misery which is the unvarying lot of the farm labourer in the South of England. His wages have scarcely risen for the last twenty years. A few of his luxuries have been cheapened. Most of the necessaries of his humble life have been made dearer, (for the development of railway communication has equalized prices in town and country,) if indeed they are not, owing to the regularity of the market, cheaper in the former than in the latter. The prices of meat, butter, cheese, and milk are at present double those at which they stood twenty years ago in rural districts. The rate of house-rent too has increased, and will it seems increase, owing to causes on which I have no time to dwell now. The best proof of the depth to which the south-country hind has descended, is to be seen in the formation of children's gangs, and in the increasingly early age at which children labour.

Cobbett, during the great war, and the reaction which followed upon peace, saw the beginning of this misery. He traced it, in some degree, to its true causes, the absorption of capital in the war, and the limited demand for labour. The wealth of the country, Cobbett thought, with some reason, was consumed in foreign expenditure, in foreign subsidies, and, in no small degree, in the profits of loan-mongers. Upon the latter functionaries he looked with intense disfavour.

Like most men of warm sympathies and warmer hatreds, Cobbett believed in the possibility of remedying these evils by communistic expedients. His 'History of the Reformation' was an attack on the hereditary wealth of the Tudor nobles. His 'Legacy to Parsons' was an assault on the endowments of the Church. His quarrels with O'Connell, his abuse of Malthus, Mr. Lowe of Bingham, and Mr. Chadwick, were the fruit of his admiration of the old poor law.

The poor law of Elizabeth was not a compensation for the loss which the people sustained by the suppression of the monasteries and the alienation of their estates. But it was a consequence of this great social change. The wealth of these orders was rapidly dissipated by Henry VIII. The price which his courtiers and grantees paid for their possessions was as rapidly squandered. Upon this waste of public capital, came the debasement of the currency, to which I have already alluded. Agriculture was abandoned, and sheep-farming substituted in its place. The peasantry was unemployed and starving. Vagrancy was made a capital offence, but ineffectually. At last a poor law was the only refuge from brigandage. Pauperism, which hardly existed during the prosperous epoch of the eighteenth century, became the prominent evil of the nineteenth. In some parishes, every shilling of rent was absorbed in the relief of the poor. It was necessary that this system should be checked, and that the remedy, however sharp it might be, should be found and applied.

Malthus and the writers of his school advocated the most extreme processes. Cobbett thought that, granting the present appropriation of the soil, and allowing that the usurpation of the landowner, as he conceived it, should be undisturbed, the poor had an inalienable right to maintenance from land. 'The right to land,' said he, 'is founded in labour, and in labour only.' Labour is divorced from the land, but it cannot be defrauded of its interest in the distribution of that which it alone has earned. To him, therefore, the arguments of these economists was not merely distasteful, but their plans were immoral and fraudulent. It was not the poor law, he thought, which had degraded the labourer, but misgovernment and reckless expenditure. It was not an attempt to better his condition by wholesome severity, which Malthus and Lowe advocated, but the relief of the landlord's rent, and the saving of the parson's tithes.

Fortunately, Cobbett and those who reasoned with him were foiled. Workhouses are no longer the warrens in which hereditary paupers are bred and brought up, but penitentiaries to the able-bodied, refuges for the aged and sick. It is true that the issue of the workhouse system is not tried by its success in discouraging the relief of capable workmen by means of a public charity. The question is yet unsettled, whether or no the agricultural labourer is not entitled to some compensation as a set-off to those laws and customs which have annihilated his interest in the soil; but no one in these days doubts that, whatever that compensation should be, it cannot and should not be a system which wholly destroys any restraint of prudence, every impulse of self-reliance and independence.

Cobbett denounced the paper money of the war, and the expedients adopted by Peel, for the resumption of cash payments after the war was over. The former had, he thought, been a great advantage to the moneyed classes, the latter was an attempt to secure the gains which the same body of financiers had accumulated during the war. With his customary rashness of political prophecy, he predicted that cash payments would never be resumed, and published his 'Gridiron' in order to sustain his views. The resumption of cash payments was necessary and just. But Cobbett was to some extent in the right. Great distress followed on the legislation of Peel. As usual, the agricultural interest suffered, was clamorous, and was heard; and we owed the latest sliding-scale to their importunities.

It would carry me far beyond the limits which time imposes on an evening lecture, if I were to attempt a fuller sketch of England at the day of Cobbett's death, and England in our own immediate present. It is sufficient to say, that though some interests have suffered—those, unhappily, which needed elevation the most,—the material progress of the country has on the whole been rapid and continuous. Prosperity has followed on wise legislation, for it is an axiom in politics, that the wage-earning classes have a far greater interest in wise government and public morality than their wealthier fellow-countrymen. The sinister predictions which accompanied the reforms of the last forty years have been falsified, and would be forgotten, were they not invariably resuscitated when other changes are demanded and impending. And above all, the United Kingdom has been fruitful in brave and wise men, whose public life has stood out in marked contrast to the Churchmen and Statesmen of Cobbett's stormy retrospect.

Again, it is not easy to discover what are the special influences which the career of such a man exerted over the age in which he lived, and over that which succeeded it. It was impossible that a popular writer, who played so notable a part on the public stage, should fail of aiding the forces out of which society has grown to its present stature and form. At least, Cobbett familiarised the people with the most effective kind of popular education, that, namely, which criticises public events and public characters. If he was not the progenitor of the free press, he was at least one of its eldest sons. It is true that he disfigured his vigorous English by personalities, and injured his own reputation by his unreasoning and ferocious animosities, but he had a hearty love for his country and his countrymen, and a readiness to strive for what he believed to be the right. For no popularity can be enduring which does not lay its foundations in a real interest for the public good, though the means may be taken in error, and the effect marred by lack of experience. In Cobbett's nature the good preponderated vastly over the evil. The influence of his writings was on the whole beneficent, for it was pure, earnest, honest. His many blemishes, both of mind and temper, prevented him from being great. The faults of his education led him into many a hasty judgment. But he kept alive much that was true and just in an age when truth and justice were reduced to struggle for existence. We may be sure that there was much that is worthy in a man whose writings were read by millions during his life, and whose coffin was followed by thousands when he was laid in the sepulchre of his fathers.

The Right Hon. John Bright's Speeches on
  Questions of Public Policy. Edited by PROFESSOR ROGERS.
  With Portrait. 2 vols. 8vo. 25s. *Second Edition.*

Lord Liverpool's Life and Administration.
  Compiled from Original Documents by PROFESSOR YONGE.
  With Portrait. 3 vols. 8vo. 42s.

The Diary, Reminiscences, and Correspondence of Henry Crabb Robinson. Selected and Edited by
  THOMAS SADLER, Ph. D. With Portrait. 3 vols. 8vo. 36s.

The Life of Sir Walter Ralegh, based upon
  Contemporary Documents. By EDWARD EDWARDS. Together with his Letters, now first Collected. With Portrait.
  2 vols. 8vo. 32s.

Miss Martineau's Biographical Sketches,
  1852-68. *Second Edition.* Containing :— The Emperor
  Nicholas—The Duchess of Kent—Joseph Hume—Lord Herbert of Lea—Lord Lansdowne—Lord Lyndhurst—Lord Palmerston—Lord Brougham—Bishop Blomfield—Archbishop
  Whately — Sir William Napier — David Roberts — Father
  Mathew—Lady Byron—Miss Mitford—Henry Hallam—Lord
  Macaulay—Mrs. Jameson, and many others. Crown 8vo.
  8s. 6d.

MACMILLAN AND CO., LONDON.

Mr. Matthew Arnold's Essays in Criticism.
New Edition revised and enlarged. Extra fcap. 8vo. 6s.

Professor Kingsley's 'The Ancien Regime.'
Lectures delivered at the Royal Institution. Crown 8vo. 6s.

Professor Masson's Essays, Biographical and Critical. Chiefly on the English Poets. 8vo. 12s. 6d.

Mr. F. T. Palgrave's Essays on Art.
Mulready—Dyce—Holman Hunt—Herbert—Poetry, Prose, and Sensationalism in Art, etc. Extra fcap. 8vo. 6s.

The Oxford Spectator. Reprinted. Extra fcap. 8vo. 3s. 6d.

Professor Bernard's Four Lectures on Subjects connected with Diplomacy. 8vo. 9s.

MACMILLAN AND CO., LONDON.

www.ingramcontent.com/pod-product-compliance
Lightning Source LLC
Chambersburg PA
CBHW020826190426
43197CB00037B/719